THE EMERGING GENERATION

THE EMERGING GENERATION

An Inside Look at Canada's Teenagers

REGINALD W. BIBBY
and
DONALD C. POSTERSKI

Irwin Publishing
Toronto   Canada

Canadian Cataloguing in Publication Data

Bibby, Reginald Wayne, 1943–
    The emerging generation: an inside look at Canada's
teenagers

Bibliography: p.
ISBN 0-7725-1522-0.

1. Youth – Canada – Attitudes. I. Posterski,
Donald C., 1942– . II. Title.

HQ799.C2B52 1985   305.2'35'0971   C85-098258-8

Text design/Robert Burgess Garbutt
Cover and inside photos/J. Fred Sharp/SHARP IMAGES

"The Logical Song", lyrics and music by Roger Hodgson and
Rick Davies, © 1979 Almo Music Corp. and Delicate Music
(ASCAP). Used by permission. International copyright secured.

Typesetting/Compeer Typographic Services Limited
Printed in Canada by Webcom Incorporated

1 2 3 4 5 6 7 8   WC   92 91 90 89 88 87 86 85

Published by Irwin Publishing Inc.

TO OUR TEENAGE TEACHERS
Reggie, Dave, Russ,
Jeff and Brenda

CONTENTS

TABLES

PREFACE

This book and the research on which it is based are the result of a number of historical accidents that brought the two authors together. Although both are originally Albertans, Posterski has been living in Toronto for the past five years, working with youth and serving as a consultant to teenage-oriented organizations. Bibby, after a stint in Toronto at York University, has been teaching for the past decade at the University of Lethbridge where he has been monitoring social trends through a series of well-known national surveys.

In 1982 Bibby was approached by a consortium of youth groups about the possibility of co-ordinating a national survey of teenagers. Posterski and Bibby subsequently began to lay the groundwork for such a survey. When the backing for the proposed survey evaporated in mid-1983, the authors decided that their initial investment warranted salvaging the project. By the end of 1983, funding had been secured. A contract with the Secretary of State for the analysis of pertinent results ensured that the costs of the project could be covered. The survey of Canadian teenagers, "Project Teen Canada", was conducted during 1984, with data collection covering the four months of May and June, September and October.

We believe that in its breadth of subject matter and extent of data "Project Teen Canada" is without precedent. An endeavour of this magnitude has clearly only been possible because of the contribution of a large number of people. First and foremost, we wish to extend our very deep appreciation to the 3,600 participating high-school students across Canada, along with the guidance counsellors and teachers who administered the survey in some 150 schools. We also had the assistance of an exceptional research assistant in Michele Cote, and further benefitted greatly from the administrative efficiency of Margaret McKeen in Lethbridge and Barb Boyt in Toronto. Debby Gordon maintained her good humour while carrying out the unenviable job of entering the large body of data. Valued also was the work of Denise Weisgerber in the designing of materials. The willingness of others to listen patiently while we tirelessly bounced results and ideas off them — Beth, Gwen, and Stan, to mention three — was additionally important to us. Finally, the work of editor D.G. Bastian, in guiding the manuscript through to its final form, has been invaluable. To all these individuals, along with the high schools, the University of Lethbridge, and the Secretary of State, we express our thanks. We are delighted that our research and this book will help raise the profile of Canadian teenagers during 1985 — International Youth Year — and beyond.

INTRODUCTION

When children are children, we know how to respond to them. When babies are hungry and cry, we feed them. When they take their first step, we stand close enough to help them stumble successfully to the second and third. When children are children, we feel safe.

When six-year-olds are six years old, we know it is time to send them to school. At home we sit them on our knees and enjoy reading Dr. Seuss books together. We kiss them good night and tuck them into bed. We like them just the way they are.

But when twelve-year-olds turn thirteen, they are less predictable, and we are less sure how to interact with them. They are changing in so many ways: their bodies, their interests, the way they treat us. Sometimes they seem to be getting out of control. As they progress through their teens, they seem to be in limbo. They no longer are children but neither are they full-fledged adults. Indeed, sociologists and psychologists generally conceive of these years as representing a period in which an individual is "lost in 'between' being a child and an adult".[1] They are adolescents.

This child–adult transitional period is filled with ambiguity. We do not allow young people to vote, drink legally, work full time, or drive on the highways until they are senior teens. Yet we ask them to make educational decisions that affect their long-term vocational futures. Teenagers have the physical and mental capabilities to commit a full range of crimes. Yet our juvenile justice system has been based on the premise that adolescents are not yet responsible for their behaviour. We recognize that physically they are now sexual beings, yet we are inclined to insist that they harness their sexuality. We know that socially they are capable of impressive moments — but then there are those other occasions. We acknowledge that mentally they can handle calculus and computers. Being rational about weekend curfews is quite another thing.

While our culture tends to stress that it is not easy to be a teenager's parent, we are taking the position in this book that it also is not easy to be a child–adult hybrid. Psychologist David Elkind has pointed out in his recent book *The Hurried Child* that North Americans seem obsessed with the need to rush their children towards adulthood. Reflecting a culture that is in a hurry, says Elkind, we force children to "take on the physical, psychological, and social trappings of adulthood before they are prepared to deal with them".[2] We expose them to education, sports, and miniature adult costumes when they are still preschoolers. The three-year-old who can read, hit the ski slopes, and wear brand-name running shoes receives enthusiastic applause. Elkind says children frequently function as status symbols, confidants, domestic workers, decision-makers, and as a means by which parents can live out their own goals; children for these adults become what he calls "surrogate selves".

Elkind proceeds to make the important point that with the coming of adolescence, marked by the onset of puberty, some "parents switch parenting styles and become authoritarian although they were once democratic."[3] The neophyte teenager, who previously was taking dancing lessons and was outfitted in designer jeans, is now told that she cannot date, regardless of how responsibly she has behaved. "Many young people who have been accustomed to dressing and talking like adults are often frustrated as adolescents because the maturity imposed upon them as children is thwarted."[4]

John Mitchell of the University of Alberta has written a provocative book, *The Adolescent Predicament*,[5] in which he claims that despite the fact that teenagers, notably those in their later teens, are capable of making significant contributions to society, we do not allow them to do so. Adolescence is largely wasted, says Mitchell, because we demand that the adolescent remain dormant, involved in trivial pastimes while staying out of trouble. "The major predicament facing adolescents in our society," he states, "is that virtually no opportunity exists to do anything (legal) which really makes a difference."

In keeping with such ideas, we believe that one of the major reasons for teenage–adult conflict is the failure of adults to be sensitive and responsive to the reality of teenage emergence. Many teenagers receive little help in growing up. Worse than that, many are discouraged from growing up. Adults cannot deny the reality of teens' physical changes and yet are unwilling to grant them equal status. Many adults simply prefer to keep teens in limbo.

Educator Richard Barbieri contends that young people "need to progress from childish gullibility, through disillusionment and doubt, to adult discernment".[6] Adolescents need to have room to develop in order to emerge as full-fledged adults; life without development is abnormal. An environment that forces a child to remain dependent denies the possibility of growth and emergence into adulthood. Such a denial is the focus of this book.

Our research has isolated several critical phenomena

directly related to the suppression of adolescent emergence. We have found that teenagers commonly perceive
adults as insensitive to their problems. Teens further indicate that they often are not taken seriously. Some go so far
as to say that an anti-adolescent mentality is fairly prevalent among adults. As a result, many feel alienated from
adults and their institutions, including the family, the school,
and the church. The results can be damaging. Psychologist
Derek Miller comments that "a distant uncomprehending
relationship between parent and adolescent, home and
school, teacher and taught, becomes menacing for the
future of society."[7]

About the Survey

In response to our survey, "Project Teen Canada", Canadian young people have given us a portrait of themselves
"from the inside". They have revealed their values, sources
of enjoyment, and personal areas of greatest concern. They
have unveiled what they believe about religion and sex.
They have given us their views on Canada. They have
told us their fears and what they expect from the future.
We are no longer in the dark on many of these subjects.
Canada's teens have spoken up.

These young people, some 3,600 in number, were scien-
tifically selected from across the country. They come from
152 randomly selected schools in Canada's five regions.
The survey was administered by guidance counsellors or
their designates. Participation was voluntary, with students
assured of anonymity and confidentiality.

Our decision to focus on teenagers aged fifteen to nineteen as opposed to teenagers as a whole was prompted by
our interest in exploring "the emerging generation" —
teenagers on the threshold of adulthood. We are well aware,
with observers like Mitchell, that there are profound differences between the lifestyles and needs of younger and
older adolescents.[8] When we speak of teens in this book,

we specifically have in mind those who are fifteen to nineteen years old. (Complete methodological details are available in the appendix.)

Our questionnaire was constructed to provide a comprehensive profile of young people regarding their attitudes, values, beliefs, outlook, expectations, and behaviour. The questionnaire was fifteen pages long and contained more than 300 items of information. It was designed, however, to be filled out with relative ease, and on the average appeared to require about 35 minutes to complete. Teens were invited to supplement the questionnaire responses with their own comments. Many did and their reflections are found throughout this book.

The 3,600 participating students together provide a sample that is sufficiently large and representative of fifteen- to nineteen-year-olds to permit highly accurate generalizations to the Canadian population. Results for a sample of this size are accurate within approximately three percentage points, nineteen surveys in twenty.

Readers interested in data analysis and the testing of hypotheses should note three brief points about the data presented in this book.

First, the findings are reported in a fairly straightforward, descriptive manner. We have tried to integrate these basic findings with previous research, rather than carry out extensive analyses within the book. Such analyses will be conducted over the next few years and will be reported in appropriate professional journals.

Second, the thesis that adolescence is a time of emergence from child to adult is being used as an interpretive framework, to "make sense" of the findings generally. No attempt is being made to carry out a *direct* empirical test of the thesis. That task also remains to be performed. Our assertion is that the thesis accounts for the facts at hand.

Third, we do not make much of regional and intraregional variations (e.g., by gender, social class). While some such analyses will be carried out in the future, we are assuming that considerable cultural levelling has occurred among those who took part in the survey. Our assumption is partly based, for example, on recent studies comparing young people in Quebec with the rest of Canada. These studies have found little differences in teens' sense of control over their lives[9] or their views on marital roles[10] and point to an intense homogenization of attitudes, beliefs, values, and practices.[11]

Our attempt to be respectable yet parsimonious in our data analysis is not without ulterior motive. We want to disseminate the results of "Project Teen Canada" to a wide Canadian audience. We think teenagers have delivered a message that needs to be heard. All of us have experienced adolescence first-hand. Virtually all of us are involved in some way with adolescents. Yet many of us did not understand clearly what we experienced during "those years". And we are often perplexed by what is happening with teenagers today. This book is written to help clear up some of the confusion.

THE EMERGING GENERATION

1

EMERGENCE

The Teenage Years

My mother never forgave me for reaching puberty.

— a fifty-six-year-old professor

The Teenage Situation: Mixed Reviews

Our national survey of Canadian teenagers provides some good news and some bad news. The good news centres on the young people themselves. Teenagers give every indication of collectively fulfilling our hopes for them. They share dominant values. They place importance on people and relationships. They want to play a significant role in national life. Says one sixteen-year-old:

> My generation has to face threats and problems that no other generation has had to face before and I think it is about time our parents and other elders knew and tried to understand this.

Most young people, although they have anxiety about their futures, are confident about themselves. A fifteen-year-old from Quebec comments:

> I believe the best way to be happy is to be yourself and
> comfortable with who you are. Just as you might envy
> someone, so might they envy you. Not very often do
> we think of ourselves as great, but we all are.

The bad news, somewhat surprisingly, relates to adults
and their role in teenagers' lives. While adults have attempted to instil ethical and moral standards, they frequently have been guilty of hypocrisy. They have demanded
more of teenagers than they have of themselves — setting,
for example, a sexual standard for teens that is quite different from the ones they have set for themselves. They have
called for racial equality yet exhibit a level of intolerance
that exceeds that of young people.

Adults have further tried to inspire dreams in their children, even though they have known all along that these
dreams are impossible for many young people to achieve.
Adults have set teenagers up for disenchantment and disappointment. Like the adults of the 1960s, the older generation will have to live with the reaction.

Perhaps most significantly, the study has underlined a
problem we believe to be the key to understanding much
of the conflict so characteristic of teenage–adult relations. It is a problem familiar to most adults, who have
experienced it first-hand. Yet, surprisingly, adults seldom
talk about it, and the media scarcely acknowledge it. It is a
problem that makes life an unhappy and sometimes very
painful experience for all children — and an especially
devastating one for adolescents.

Stated simply, the problem is *the failure of adults to let
young people grow up*. Expressed another way, *adults suppress emergence*. The problem surfaces over and over again.
As a sixteen-year-old from southern Alberta says:

> Many adults misunderstand teenagers. They think they
> are into drugs, sex and alcohol. Well, most of us are not.
> They also think we're irresponsible. Well, some are,
> but most are not. I hope when our generation grows up

and has kids we will give the teenagers a fair chance compared to this adult generation we have now.

A sixteen-year-old young man from Newfoundland speaks on behalf of many other teens:

I wish teenagers' opinions were taken more seriously, especially on political matters. Like females a hundred years ago, we are a minority group. Maybe in a hundred years' time, teens will have the vote and other rights.

An eighteen-year-old from the west coast was even more graphic in his comments:

I've been a teenager for five years and [this is] the first time I've been asked what I thought about anything other than drugs.

Because the emergence problem is central to interpreting the survey findings, it bears closer examination.

Two Versions of the Same Story

The teenage years are often far from "a blessed event" for all concerned. For parents and other adults, these are seen as the "storm and stress years". Conflict and strain are regarded as virtually inevitable, as constituting "the costs" parents must absorb if they choose to have children. Many a parent has spoken of "dreading" these years. At their conclusion, battle-weary mothers and fathers gain some consolation from the fact that they are finally over. The adult interpretation of the teenage experience is well known. It tends to go something like this . . .

The Adult Version

In their teenage years, sons and daughters who were a source of delight to their parents and other adults are seemingly transformed. They go from being warm and open to being detached and non-communicative. When they do speak they are often curt or evasive. It is difficult to get straight answers from them. They often are rude and insensitive to the feelings of parents and other people. They commonly insist on having their own privacy or prefer to do things with their friends rather than with the rest of family. Parents often wonder, "Where do they get those friends, anyway?"

It is difficult to tell teens anything, the adult version goes, because they suddenly think they know everything. They want all kinds of freedom, but they don't want to accept responsibility. Teenagers think only about having fun — music, parties, and dating. They are self-centred. They don't take school or life seriously. And they are always asking for money. Teenagers are the source of considerable anxiety, anguish, and pain. They occasionally get into trouble at school and may even have a brush with the police. Sometimes they are a source of embarrassment. Then there's the problem of alcohol and drugs and sex. Often teens seem to be out of control. Adults don't know what will become of them. At times mothers and fathers long for the early days when their teenagers were young and adorable and manageable. Sometimes they simply wish that they had never had children.

But parents are told by those who have gone before them that they must try to be patient and understanding. The experts remind them that the adolescent period is the product of their children's "developmental status, their limited environment, and their changing bodies".[1] They are told that, for most teenagers, the transformation into the "terrible teens" gives way to a further transformation. By the time young people reach their late teens or early twenties, they have adjusted to their new-found adult status. Almost miraculously, they again become normal, civil, and enjoyable. They realize how much their parents really knew.

Hang on, parents are urged, for many sons and daughters will eventually tell you, "Mom and Dad, I don't know how you ever put up with me." And mothers and fathers will sigh with relief, regarding the whole experience as one they could have nicely done without.

Obviously this is only a crude outline of the adult version. But the basic story-line is this: for a period of years, many young people aren't quite human. As someone has put it, parents feel they are working not with a "generation gap" but a "species gap". Yet parents and other adults are told they must see these recalcitrant teenagers through their difficult time. Eventually teens will "come around", giving the story a happy ending.

The problem with such a "tears and cheers" account is that it is told strictly from the viewpoint of adults. It is believable because it is offered by credible people — adults — and seemingly accounts for the facts at hand. However, the perceptions of teenagers are blatantly absent from this version. Let us look, for a moment, at those same "facts" from the vantage-point of the young person . . .

The Teenage Version

These teenage years are exciting, but they have to be the most difficult years, teenagers may be heard to say. The cards are stacked against them. Society seems to assume that parents are perfect, or nearly always so. Teachers, group leaders, employers, the police, and ministers or priests are also seen as always right, strictly because they're adults.

When teenagers were younger and obviously different from grown-ups, adults felt safer. After all, children can be held and hugged, directed and disciplined. They know little and question much. Their lives are controlled by adults. How and where they spend their time is determined by parents. They are told how to dress, what to say, and how to act. Sex is tightly locked behind adult bedroom doors. Children are treated not as equals but as possessions. Other adults refer to them as someone's children; their mother and father call them *my* baby, *my* son, and *my* daughter.

But when they begin to become adults, things change. Many parents and other adults seem to resent the fact that they are growing up and want to continue to treat them like children. When they question and disagree, they are treated as brash and rude, and even as troublemakers. Teenagers still want to hold and hug, but no longer in the role of "lovable little kids". They want to be given suggestions and guidelines, not ordered around like soldiers or treated like poodles on the end of adult leashes.

Older people say teens can't be told anything. But part of the problem is that they are learning a great deal and would like to have a chance to share what they know, rather than having to be constantly educated by adults whose own knowledge is questionable. Socially many of them are becoming more adept than parents, often because of their exposure to a greater diversity of lifestyles. Physically they are moving into "prime time", precisely when many parents and adults are being dismissed from it. Teenagers are discovering and exploring sexuality. They are beginning to sense their own individuality, rather than seeing themselves as simply belonging to other people. So they are led to question how they became what they are, and to ponder what they will yet become.

However, many parents typically won't "let" teenagers grow up. Adults make it tough to be a teenager. They either actively resist their movement into adulthood or simply are unable to cope with it. They commonly want to play by the irrelevant rules of childhood,

- giving orders instead of inviting discussion,
- demanding that private thoughts and events be unveiled,
- forcing "allegiance showdowns" over time spent with friends versus family,

- insisting on time accountability,
- imposing the accusation of selfishness on us when parents' wishes are resisted.

And then, of course, they constantly worry,

- about how teens spend their time, and about how they don't spend their time,
- about what they will become, and about what they might not become.
- They worry when teens have friends, and when they don't have friends.
- They worry when teens spend time with the opposite sex, and when they spend time with the same sex.

The Nature of Emergence

The teenage version points to the extreme difficulty many adults have in recognizing and responding to teenage emergence. Just what is emergence? To live is to emerge, to constantly become something new. A sampling of the video frames of a typical biography summarizes the story. A baby gives way to a toddler, who by the first day of school is transformed into a talkative, curious youngster. That budding person has largely disappeared by the end of grade six, with the appearance and lifestyle of the replacement in turn scarcely recognizable on high-school graduation day. Emergence continues as one prepares for a career, becomes part of the labour force, marries, and has children. A frame of the high-school reunion, like the reading of an old diary, is a succinct and poignant reminder that the physical, social, and psychological ties between past and present are precarious. Former classmates look different, act different, feel different, and *are* different. Yet the video is not finished. Further frames reveal the emergence of a greying individual, grandchildren, retirement and, finally, one's imminent entry into the most mysterious of all zones — death. Looking back, it is apparent that the primary link with the past is probably only *memory*.[2]

Life is emergence, continuous becoming. We do not merely get old; we constantly are becoming something new. The teenage years are consequently not novel in representing emergence. They are, however, of deep significance because they signify the time when young people are becoming full-fledged human beings. After more than a decade of being treated as "premature adults" — regarded as inferior experientially, physically, intellectually, socially, emotionally, and spiritually — teenagers are becoming like the people who, until now, have claimed superiority and exercised control. They are experiencing a multi-dimensional transformation that signals their farewell to childhood.

This movement from child to adult has not been made easier by the social creation of "adolescence". People frequently confuse "adolescence" with "puberty". While puberty refers to a specific period of physical growth and sexual maturation, adolescence is a term coined to mark the period from puberty's onset to the beginning of adulthood. Interestingly, such anthropologists as Margaret Mead and Ruth Benedict have argued that in many cultures there is no radical break as one moves from childhood to adulthood. It is a smooth, "continuous" process.[3] Indeed, children in virtually all societies used to become adults without going through "adolescence".[4] Teens were expected to get married and support themselves at an early age. But with the Industrial Revolution came advanced technology and the need for longer schooling. As a result, the time between biological maturity and recognition of adult status was lengthened; the term "adolescence" has been invented to describe this period of limbo in which young people are neither children nor adults.

Of central importance is the fact that emergence from this hybrid adolescent stage, along with emergence more generally, involves far more than one's own initiative and abilities. People do not evolve in a social vacuum. Others profoundly influence the process. Sometimes — as with parents, a marriage partner, or close friends — this is because they have primary roles in our lives. In other instances, other people's impact on our emergence is tied to the authority they have over us, as is the case with teachers, police officers, and religious leaders.

In the Middle Ages, jesters were sometimes created by putting young children in boxes and force-feeding them. As they grew, their bones would warp in unusual (and entertaining) shapes.[5] To varying degrees, we all have encountered individuals who have had both positive and negative influences on our emergence. We variously commend and indict a parent, a teacher, a husband, a minister, an employer, a friend. Some inspired our development; others retarded it. Some "helped us grow"; others "kept us down". Unfortunately, parents are often among the chief box-keeping culprits. Adults can either facilitate emergence or make it more difficult.

A more detailed description of teenage emergence will be a part of our conclusions in Chapter Ten. In particular, we will outline there the suppression of emergence by adults and adult institutions and propose a method of parent–teen co-operation in the emergence process. Our study is not offered as a "how to" manual for parents on "training" teens. But we believe our conclusions will reduce adult fear levels about adolescence and provide guidance for relating with teenagers. Neither is it our intent to lay out a blueprint for adolescents to follow during their teenage years. However, we hope our observations and recommendations will assist young people to understand themselves better as they move into their futures.

First, however, we want to listen to what Canada's teenagers themselves have to say about their values, pleasures, concerns, and expectations.

2 VALUES:

What Is Important to Teenagers

Things have changed on the surface for us, but otherwise we are the same as our adults were when they were young.

— an eighteen-year-old female

Values and Their Sources

Late in 1984 a group of 27 American educationists and scholars issued a Thanksgiving Statement expressing alarm over "soaring rates of teenage homicides, suicides, and out-of-wedlock births". These rates, they said, had risen more quickly than those of adults. The group attacked schools in the United States for being silent and timid about instilling good character traits. The group called for a correction of the situation, through steps ranging from more rigorous grading and better discipline to subsidies for competitive, private schools.[1]

The lament is not new. A major concern that seems to be expressed about every coming generation centres on values. Society seems almost paranoid about the possibility that the next generation will somehow reject the

13

aspects of life their parents and grandparents claim to cherish most. Every new generation is anxiously viewed as more decadent and less responsible than the previous ones.

Take, for example, such a time-honoured value as honesty. In a 1968 Gallup Poll, 44% of Canadians said they felt honesty was deteriorating in the country. Only 13% said they felt it was on the upswing. In 1982 an even higher proportion, 66%, viewed honesty as on the decline, with only 11% maintaining that it was actually increasing.[2]

It is doubtful that a new generation has *ever* been seen as possessing a superior level of value endorsement by an earlier generational cohort. Such vindications seem to be the exclusive prerogative of historians. Educator Anthony Kerr has said, "I have a pretty fair idea of History over the past twenty-five centuries and cannot recall a time when the old were fully satisfied with the young . . . And yet the world has gone on, apparently getting no worse."[3] Our findings, in the main, support Kerr's position.

The Canadian Situation

Social psychologist Milton Rokeach, who taught for a time at the University of Western Ontario, has carried out extensive research on values helpful to our present quest. He has identified two types of values: *terminal values* and *instrumental* values. Terminal values represent the end-states an individual would like to reach. Instrumental values represent the preferred ways of pursuing those end-states.[4]

We asked Canadian teenagers to rate the importance of some of these values. Eight terminal values were drawn from Rokeach's work: a comfortable life, excitement, family life, freedom, friendship, acceptance by God, being loved, and recognition. (Rokeach's actual value for acceptance by God is "salvation"; we found this too nebulous for our purposes.) We also added three values that we felt might be particularly pertinent to young people: being popular, privacy, and success. Similarly, eight of Rokeach's instrumental values were used: cleanliness, forgiveness, honesty, imagination, intelligence, politeness, reliability, and hard work.

The reader does not have to be familiar with the social psychologist's writings to recognize that he has isolated sentiments that are highly valued in our society. But to what extent do Canada's teenagers also view them as important?

Terminal, "End-State" Values

Friendship and Love. In keeping with the value placed on relationships and love in our culture generally, friendship and being loved are the two traits valued most by Canadian teenagers (see Table 2.1). Such findings point not to cold and callous young people who are beyond the emotional reach of adults who care. They rather indicate that behind the exteriors of adolescents who sometimes seem independent and emotionally indifferent are people who very much want companionship and a sense that they matter to someone. For example, a seventeen-year-old young woman from the Maritimes declares:

> I can't stand the coldness of people and their [impersonal ways of relating]. There seems to be little warmth and a large lack of understanding.

The point is forcefully stated by a grade ten teenager from Quebec:

> Love will make all the difference. The delinquents are those who rebel. That is mainly the result of a lack of understanding and loving. So let us love each other and the future will be built.

A sixteen-year-old male from northern Ontario expresses the same sentiment:

Teenagers now should listen to their parents more so that you get more. By more I don't mean concrete things like bikes and clothes but I mean love, love between each other instead of misunderstanding and hatred.

John Mitchell has pointed out that "part of our image of the superyouth is one who is aloof, detached, and beyond the petty inconveniences of deep emotion and alert sensitivity." He adds that "the frenzied obsession with the present . . . represents, for many of them, an attempt to stave off the recurring impulse for intimacy relationships."[5] Elkind comments: "What needs to be kept in mind is that adolescents still care about their parents and want to be cared about."[6] In the words of one Ottawa-area fifteen-year-old:

A person will go to almost any lengths to feel or be loved. Believe me, I know.

The battered old cliché, "looks are deceiving," has application here.

Freedom.   The third foremost-held value, reflecting the reality of teenage emergence, is freedom. Teens are acutely aware that they need room to live and grow.

Such a valuing of freedom to emerge should not be confused with a desire to irresponsibly "do anything you want". That interpretation of the desire for freedom by teenagers has for too long been popularized by adults who have forgotten.

We cannot live out our own individuality if we do not have freedom to think our own thoughts and do what we want. To find that another human being insists on controlling one's ideas and one's behaviour when one wants to control them for oneself is overwhelmingly painful. Few teenagers welcome such claustrophobia — nor did we when we were in the process of becoming adults.

Today's teenagers are indeed no different. As one sixteen-year-old Quebec male points out:

Freedom is something every human being wants.

TABLE 2.1 *Terminal Values by Region:*

% Viewing as "Very Important"

	Nationally	B.C.	Prairies	Ontario	Quebec	Atlantic
Friendship	91	91	92	91	90	92
Being Loved	87	83	86	87	88	89
Freedom	84	87	83	86	81	87
Success	78	82	76	80	75	79
A Comfortable Life	75	77	70	82	68	78
Privacy	68	68	66	69	67	70
Family Life	65	64	66	70	59	67
Excitement	58	62	57	66	47	60
Acceptance by God	41	33	48	47	27	49
Recognition	41	33	37	42	49	36
Being Popular	21	21	19	24	19	23

Young people want the freedom to emerge, room to become what they are capable of being. The unreasonable suppression of their freedom "to become" will understandably be a source of discomfort and potential conflict. With uninhibited idealism, a grade twelve francophone female from a rural Quebec community comments:

> We teenagers want to be free. Let us face life on our own, and we'll find our own solutions. You can take care of us by creating more activities and jobs for us. We need them. But we can take care of ourselves.

Success and Comfort. Ranking fourth and fifth, and seen as very important by three in four teenagers, are "success in what I do" and "a comfortable life". Canadian young people value the idea of doing well the things they consider to be important. They strive for excellence in the activities they perceive *themselves* as "doing". Parents are often concerned that teens are not committed to quality performance. They are probably presupposing the activities they deem appropriate for their children. True, young people may not be committed to getting top grades or helping around the house. But that is hardly to say that they lack motivation. Their trains are usually moving very well, but they are on different sets of track. The task for adults is not one of implanting the desire for success, but rather one of encouraging success on the tracks they regard as having *primary* importance.

The comfortable life? Who does not want it? Even the drop-outs from society would like to have the satisfaction of at least being able to turn their backs on it. Still, for all the talk about our nation's obsession with materialism, it is important to keep in mind that "the good life" is not as commonly valued by adolescents as are good and fulfilling relationships.

Privacy.　In sixth place in the value rankings, endorsed by about 70%, is privacy. Its high ranking should come as no surprise. Privacy is a key component of freedom. It allows people to be alone with their own thoughts. This is why teenagers need their own physical space, and the freedom to treat it how they please. The eternal conflict with parents over "a messy room" has little to do with sanitation. It has everything to do with freedom and privacy.

Paul Copus, a professor of psychiatry at the University of Alberta, is among those who concur. Copus told the 1984 annual meeting of the Canadian Medical Association that teens whose bedrooms dismay their parents are simply staking out their territorial rights like any young animal. "They are demonstrating this by keeping their rooms as they like them, which is exactly the way parents don't want."[7]

Beyond providing us with the privilege of being alone when we so choose, privacy further allows us to regulate which people we will associate with. This is why teenagers resent being told who they should befriend, or being ordered to divulge all the personal details of what they have just done or plan to do. Such accountability is often debilitating and humiliating for any human being. It is often resisted. Emerging teenagers are no exception.

Excitement.   A life characterized by excitement is highly valued by almost 6 in 10 young people. One seventeen-year-old female from a coastal town in British Columbia captures the mood:

> I think you could have had more questions about DRUGS, SEX, and ROCK because that's all kids think about.

While excitement clearly is important to many teens, as it is to many adults, it is vastly overrated. It is true that young people want to have thrills. They want to have fun. But excitement takes a back seat to the less spectacular features of life, namely companionship and love. Compared with those values, excitement is a secondary issue.

God and Recognition.   A minority, only about 40%, view "acceptance by God" and recognition as very important. Such a finding suggests that acceptance and recognition by valued friends is more important for many than either being religious or being acknowledged by people in general. We will return to religion and recognition questions later.

Popularity.   Similarly, in contrast to our cultural stereotype, only a small proportion of teens (21%) place great importance on being popular. Being accepted and respected by one's own "reference group" — the group whose ideas are decisive for us — is apparently more significant than leading or pleasing "the crowd". Today's teens are more attracted to close relationships than they are to the acclaim of their peers. A large majority would rather experience acceptance and a sense of intimacy with their friends than be president of the student council. This may well represent a new trend among young people, in part reflecting a waning of conventionalism and a rise of individualism.[8]

Family Life.   This remaining terminal value warrants special attention. Despite the value placed on the family in Canadian society, only 65% of teenagers report that it is "very important" to them. Given that almost 90% say that they highly value friendship and being loved, we would suggest that these findings indicate that, during these years at least, the family is failing to function as a source of happiness, compassion, and love for many Canadian young people.

Some will respond, "That's to be expected. These are the years when they turn to their friends, and for the time being, downplay the importance of their families." Agreed. But if that is all that is happening, there is no reason why the valuing of friendship should be at the expense of valuing one's family life. Gratification from both should ideally be complementary, *if* both are significant sources of enjoyment. But as we will see in Chapter Three, such is not the case.

Instrumental, "Preferred Means" Values

Honesty.   When it comes to values pertaining to how life should be lived, Canadian young people mirror conventional ideas. Despite the concern of adults that honesty is declining, it is viewed as very important by 85% of teenagers. Here, the danger of adult hypocrisy is readily apparent. Adolescents are being taught the importance of being honest. Yet as the two aforementioned polls probing the perception of honesty indicate, adults clearly are sufficiently dishonest in their dealings with each other to be well aware that honesty is precariously practised.

Middle-Class Virtues.   Teenagers also indicate that they strongly endorse what have come to be known as "the

TABLE 2.2 *Instrumental Values by Region:*

% Viewing as "Very Important"

	Nationally	B.C.	Prairies	Ontario	Quebec	Atlantic
Honesty	85	78	87	86	83	88
Cleanliness	79	74	72	81	81	83
Working Hard	69	73	68	73	63	72
Reliability	68	73	75	78	45	71
Forgiveness	67	65	78	76	44	73
Politeness	65	67	65	72	51	70
Intelligence	63	64	60	66	60	67
Imagination	41	47	37	42	43	36

typical middle-class virtues", namely cleanliness, reliability, hard work, and intelligence (see Table 2.2). They also tend to place a high value on the social graces of politeness and forgiveness.

Thus the ideals that historically have been seen as central to the Canadian social system — rationality and industry, ethical dealings and consideration for others, conscientiousness and clean living — appear to be firmly entrenched among members of the emerging generation.

Imagination. The placement of imagination as the least appreciated value is alarming. Only 4 out of 10 teens ascribe high levels of importance to being imaginative. In the minds of the majority of young people, being truthful and clean-cut is more crucial than being creative. It leads one to wonder what happens to the imaginative dispositions of toddlers and preschoolers. What have teenagers picked up from our culture that has caused them to discount imaginativeness?

Much has been written charging our school systems with having stifled rather than stimulated creativity in young people. Television has also come in for its fair share of blame. Watching TV, social critics point out, is a passive and non-expressive activity. Turning the channel finder or pressing the selector switch hardly qualifies as a creative act. And most of what they see is mundane. Television programmers are renowned for discovering successful formulas that are then copied by other programmers — with only a few variables of place and faces changed — again and again.

Also culpable may be the importance to many teens, and perhaps to their parents, of holding down a part-time job during the school year. Where an earlier generation perhaps had more free time for artistic and group activities, more of today's teens head from the school for after-hours' jobs that hardly encourage creativity. Just to pick one industry, a "starter job" for many teens is working in a McDonald's or Harvey's or one of a host of other fast-food stores. The key to such operations is to find a formula that is successful and then to repeat it with exactness, all the while programming customers to count on consistency. Making a technological hamburger with a touch of imagination is not only discouraged, it is unacceptable.

One cannot help but wonder if something uniquely human has somehow been lost along the way from childhood to the teen years. Supertramp describes the process aptly:

> When I was young, it seemed that life was so
> Wonderful, a miracle, oh it was beautiful, magical.
> And all the birds in the trees, well they'd be singing so
> Happily, joyfully, playfully, watching me.
> But then they sent me away to teach me how to be
> Sensible, logical, responsible, practical.
> And they showed me a world where I could be so
> Dependable, clinical, intellectual, cynical.
> . . . Won't you please, please tell me what we've learned.[9]

Assessment

Despite the predictable anxiety on the part of adults about value changes, any dramatic inter-generational changes in values would be surprising. The reason is simple. As University of Waterloo sociologist Frank Fasick puts it, "Parents, the school, the church and the community at large nearly always seek to instill in young persons a commitment to the values, the norms and the customs that form the existing social order . . . Value autonomy must be rare if social stability is to be maintained."[10] Moreover, our major institutions have been highly successful historically in transmitting dominant values and discouraging value dissonance. Consequently, most Canadians and Americans, for example, make fairly predictable value selections from fairly old value menus.

An apparent exception, the youth of the 1960s, provides an interesting case study. In the U.S., Canada, and various Western European countries, the media portrayed young people as disillusioned with adult values and institutions, advocating a counter-culture, and preparing to carry out political revolution.

Yet, as one such observer later acknowledged, "I had neglected to note that while their countercultural colleagues were making news in the streets, the great majority of youth were back home working, going to school, and making their grades. Usually overlooked in the news media, these kids were still enrolling in college courses and sweating through a degree . . . still worrying about getting jobs after graduation, still being drafted, and generally taking their place in the traditional nine-to-five society."[11] He adds that a public opinion poll at the end of the 1960s found that American college students "most admired", in order, Edmund Muskie, Richard Nixon, Ted Kennedy, and Billy Graham!

We do not mean to minimize the potential of youth minorities to have a cultural and political impact on our societies. However, we would underscore the fact that even in this period of such publicized societal disaffection on the part of youth, the values and related lifestyles of the majority of young people were largely untouched.[12]

It is also interesting to note with Canadian sociologist

Kenneth Westhues that the protests of students in Canada and elsewhere reflected "a basic demand by youth to be able to live out the values of creativity, independence, and autonomy", which, he writes and we would emphasize, "they had learned from their society."[13] Even here, concern was expressed not over the nature of transmitted values, but over the failure of their implementation. Indeed, researchers found that the parents of political radicals were usually political liberals themselves.[14]

In short, adult institutions have a powerful influence on the value formation of young people. Canada is no exception.

Our survey has found that those terminal and instrumental values deemed most important by adult Canadians are also held by a solid majority of young people. Analyses by regions of the country, as reported, along with gender and community size, have revealed only minor variations. Such a pattern of value continuity between generations is similar to what has been found in the U.S. by American researchers.[15] With adult standards as criteria for judgement, the summation of a grade ten female from the Toronto area seems accurate:

> My generation is a good generation. We are not any worse or any more rebellious than our elders were at our age.

Research to date supports that position. The majority of studies that focus on "normal" adolescents agree that most are not problems, not in turmoil, not deeply disturbed, not at the mercy of their impulses, not rebellious, and not resistant to parental values.[16] So far as values go, the survey findings support the assertion of U.S. family experts Flake-Hobson, Robinson, and Skeen: "The idea that there was or is a wide generation gap between the majority of adolescents and adults in our society is simply a myth."[17] What differences in outlook do exist, they suggest, are related more to factors such as social class and religion, rather than age.

The observation of Canadian legal researcher Daniel Baum on the heels of the explosive 60s seems applicable today: "It seems that all is quiet, that youth has slipped back into their assigned place."[18] This is not the Golden Age for dissidents. The musical poetry of David Bowie, in his song, "1984", reveals the plight of the 60s rebel who in the 80s is without a cause: "I'm looking for the treason that I knew in '65."[19]

But there are some problem signs. Value continuity is apparent, but Canadians in this age group indicate some reservations about family life. Somehow, the family appears to have difficulty complementing the freedom-mindedness of emerging teenagers, even though, ironically and perhaps tragically, young people so highly value companionship and love.

For adolescents, friendship and freedom are the most desirable dancing partners, setting up the key emergence battle that takes place in the home. Teenagers assert themselves in their families by chasing after both values at the same time. Parents, meanwhile, often feel they have been shunted to the sidelines. They watch with a strong desire to cut in and ask for the next dance. Many parents find resisting the temptation to meddle in the friendship department almost impossible. Many battles are fought over who should and who should not be a friend. Parents are worried about the influence of other teens on their children. Teenagers view the interference as an assault on their autonomy. Accusations about "not trusting me" and "you are treating me like a child" turn many meals into shouting matches.

The cramping of teen style in the emerging process is taken up in the larger sphere by institutions. In dealing with emergence, our institutions give evidence of effectively carrying out the task of instilling dominant values necessary for "participant membership" in Canadian society. However, they also give preliminary evidence of often failing to explore and encourage individual potential. Youth therapist Ted Clark's assessment of "the typical teenager" serves to warn us about the kind of person we may be "producing": "[He] has few opinions that are based on personal experience, reflection, or scholarship. Rather, his opinions are what the young person believes will be acceptable to authority . . . Few can think, 'Like a magpie, the child's mind picks up bits and pieces of data. . . . They lack imagination and creativity and seem to be oriented toward finding out what is expected of them and doing that . . . They lack a sense of self; they have nothing to say."[20]

The assessment is not limited to academic circles. *The Who* have succinctly set it to music: "Any kid can chatter, few can inform."[21]

Among the potential tragedies of the failure to credit imagination and innovation adequately is the inability to respond creatively to social and personal problems. Twenty-five years ago, Paul Goodman, in *Growing Up Absurd,* noted that people have become so absorbed with the intricacies of institutional inter-relationships that they have ceased to be able to imagine alternatives. "We seem," he says, "to have lost our genius for inventing changes to satisfy crying needs."[22]

3

ENJOYMENT:

What Makes Teenagers Happy

I think the most important part of your life is your friends. They can relate to you unlike your parents can.

— *a grade twelve female from Regina*

Major Sources of Happiness

While working on this project one of the authors escaped for a brief Florida vacation. One afternoon while he was indulging in the sun and sand, two teenagers caught his attention. They were walking with a lot of energy and every now and then they included an extra dance step in their stride. As they came closer, the reason for their vitality became clear. Both had headphones on. A double patch cord from a Walkman was linking them together. Their music was giving them the same sound experience. They were oblivious to anything else around them. They had what they wanted. They were with each other and their music.

These two teens on the beach were doing what the majority of young people enjoy most. *They were close to a friend and tuned into their music.*

Relationships

In keeping with the value placed on friendship, love, and freedom, the survey has found that teenagers across Canada receive their greatest amount of enjoyment from two areas: *relationships* and *music*. More than 7 in 10 maintain that they experience "a great deal" of enjoyment from friendships.

Significantly, more than half of the country's adolescents maintain that they receive high levels of enjoyment from relationships involving a boy-friend or girl-friend or dating (see Table 3.1). Such a finding is consistent with other research. One study of 1,000 U.S. adolescents found that half of twelve- and thirteen-year-olds felt that they had been in love in the past two years, while two-thirds of sixteen- and seventeen-year-olds reported being in love during the past year.[1]

While we are all well aware that these trial-and-error relationships with the opposite sex vacillate between bringing ecstasy and agony, "at best", according to rock group Atlantic Starr, their importance to young people alienated from the adult world should not be taken lightly. Loneliness and vulnerability can be countered with the strength of another, and "with this strength I can go on."[2]

The other people who have contact with teens on a regular basis do not fare so well. Fewer than half of Canadian adolescents claim high levels of enjoyment from relating to their parents. Although mothers slightly edge out fathers in this category, the overall rating reveals that only about 4 in 10 teenagers get "a great deal" of personal enjoyment from parental relationships. As one grade twelve teenager notes:

> I think the family role is not as important as it should be. Mothers, fathers, and kids aren't as close as they should be. This situation takes away from the fun that kids have with their friends and makes [for] added worries.

A common lament among parents is that the one who has to be the more active in disciplining offspring is also more likely to be on the receiving end of their wrath. "Discipline," so they say, "is a thankless task." Research indicates that the Canadian pattern is for mothers to be more lenient towards boys and fathers to be more lenient towards girls.[3] One would logically predict that if the "discipline–no thanks" thesis is accurate, by the time of adolescence, boys would lean towards mothers, girls towards fathers.

According to our survey, however, such is not the case. Young males are only slightly more likely to claim high gratification from mothers (43%) than fathers (40%), while females actually show a tendency to know more enjoyment from mothers than from fathers (49% vs. 38%). Sisters and brothers, along with grandparents, fall further down the scale for teens as a whole. Nationally, only 1 in 4 claim high levels of enjoyment from these extensions of the family circle. In part, of course, this is because some do not have grandparents (only 5% do not have a brother or sister).

These sibling–grandparent findings are not really surprising. While brothers and sisters often provide companionship, affection, and information, they also can be a source of stress. Research conducted by Walter Toman, for example, indicates that siblings six or more years apart tend to grow up like single children. When there is less than six years' difference between them, the children are often a threat to each other's power and command over their parents. He concludes that the closer in age they are, the more severe the conflict. Yet in later life, says Toman, those close in age are emotionally closer to each other than is the case with age-spaced siblings.[4] Grandparents and adolescents frequently experience some uneasiness, due in part to the inclination of some grandparents to assume an active role in the rearing of their offspring's children. One commentator goes so far as to say that "it is

TABLE 3.1 *Sources of Enjoyment:*

"How much enjoyment do you receive from the following?"

% *Reporting "A Great Deal"*

	Nationally	B.C.	Prairies	Ontario	Quebec	Atlantic
Friendships	74	77	77	77	68	75
Music	72	81	71	79	61	72
Boy-friend/Girl-friend	55	54	50	56	56	57
Dating	50	48	49	54	44	53
Your stereo	47	58	46	53	35	48
Your mother	46	46	39	47	53	42
Sports	44	44	42	46	43	41
Your father	39	40	33	40	44	35
Television	29	30	27	31	26	36
Your grandparents	28	29	28	29	27	29
Brother(s)	26	24	23	29	27	24
Sister(s)	26	28	20	27	28	25
Your car	22	25	25	24	18	18
Your job	20	17	15	19	26	14
School	15	17	11	17	15	16
Youth groups	11	10	10	10	12	13
Church (or synagogue) life	8	7	8	9	6	11

a rare grandparent who achieves the right degree of help-ing without interfering."[5] As adolescents get older, they are inclined again to accept grandparents more graciously. Grandparents frequently reciprocate.

Music

The importance of music to teenagers can hardly be over-stated. It is a major path to both happiness and freedom.

About 7 in 10 say that music is a central source of enjoyment, with one half specifically claiming high levels of gratification from their stereos (see Table 3.1). As an activity option, music has no equal. Some 90% of teens say that they listen to music "very often". Only 1% contend that they "seldom" or "never" come under the spell of a musical experience. One seventeen-year-old teenager from Saskatoon acknowledges the place of music in his life:

> Music plays an important part in my life. I'm really into heavy metal. My parents give me a rough time. Their parents didn't like Elvis or rock 'n' roll when it just came out, but they listened to it anyways, and it didn't affect them. Hard rock is being put down by them now, but I don't think it will seriously affect us.

It is estimated that teenagers spend an average of six hours a day listening to music on their radios and stereos.[6] Some of this time or perhaps additional time is now spent watching rock videos, which have been experiencing explosive growth. Researchers tell us that the very popularity of teenagers frequently depends on their familiarity with and use of popular music.[7]

By comparison, about 60% of adults claim they listen to music "very often".[8] But it is also seven times more likely that for adults the music will provide "background" for another activity. It more commonly is "centre stage" for teenagers.[9] These kinds of findings reflect the Canadian world we know. A walk down a typical street brings our ears into contact with an unrestrained stereo sharing a bass beat with the world. A paper boy wearing headphones has a Walkman clipped to his belt. A group of young people talk and laugh to the sound of a ghetto blaster counting down the week's top 30. In the car, in the park, in the weight room, the story is the same.

And then there are the rock concerts. The Jackson Brothers' Victory Tour of 55 concerts in 20 cities hit Montreal, Toronto, and Vancouver in 1984 and played to packed stadiums. Tickets sold for $40 each, with the demand so great that sales in Montreal, for example, were limited to twelve per customer. Yet a tour spokesman claimed, "As outrageous as this may sound, this is a very inexpensive ticket for what the audience will get. They will hear sound which is crystal clear. They will see the perspiration on the artists' brows . . . They will see the greatest entertainment spectacle of all time."[10] He didn't appear to be exaggerating. A Canadian Press account following the two Montreal concerts described them this way:

> . . . the two concerts here were exactly as touted — a show to remember . . . Inside the cavernous stadium, the crowd roared its approval as Jackie, Jermaine, Marlon, Randy, Tito and their superstar kid brother, 26-year-old Michael, put on the dazzling high-tech spectacle the tour has become famous for . . . And indeed the concert — featuring exploding smoke bombs, colored laser beams that shot out across the stadium, robotic monsters and a seven-storey high stage — was spectacular. Michael remained the focal point throughout the carefully scripted concerts, dazzling the crowd with his extraordinarily fluid dancing and his famous moonwalk . . .[11]

Music is unparalleled as a medium that captivates young people. To live in a family with teenagers is to find oneself wondering, How can someone who always sleeps in miraculously rise at 6.00 a.m. on a Saturday to stand in line for rock concert tickets? How can they keep watching those same rock videos they've seen a hundred times before? Why is it impossible to drive anywhere without a teenager reaching for the radio? Where do those tapes and posters keep coming from? How do they manage to memorize lyrics we can't even make out? And why does their music always have to be so loud?

While we occasionally puzzle and wince, most of us know the experience well. Michael Jackson and Boy George may not be Elvis Presley or Pat Boone. Mötley Crüe, Van

Halen, and the Sex Pistols are definitely not The Platters, the Everly Brothers, or The Diamonds. But our memories tell a similar story of those adolescent days when we "discovered" popular music.

Music's presence, popularity, and power among young people can, in part at least, be understood in the light of their emergence into adulthood. It symbolizes *energy* and *release* and *freedom*.

For young people, music is like the engine in a Formula I racing car running in neutral at high RPMs. The musicians are the drivers who shift the gears and rev the motors. Young people are the passengers along for the joy ride. The closer they can get to the drivers the more pleasurable the ride. The drivers experiment, going faster and driving wilder. There are no laws or limits. They push for their own excitement and the ecstasy of those along. They are ready to try anything to sense something higher. No risk is too great to experience the ultimate ride. Music is *an energizing experience*.

Emotions are aroused. They cannot stay still. They mimic their heroes as they listen to their records. They project themselves as the drivers. They dance inside and out. They have a psychic encounter with themselves and their environment. They are emotionally stimulated. They are sensually stimulated. They feel good. Music is *an experience of ecstatic personal release*.

Music is also *an expression of freedom* for young people. Their distinct musical world stands as a symbol of their independence. They own a reality that belongs to them. Adults are left as onlookers trying to figure out what is happening. Walkmans, equipped with headphones, are a statement of individual freedom. The quickest way to tune out the world and go "solo" is simply to put in a tape and press the play button. An eighteen-year-old from Toronto sums it all up:

> The records, concerts, lights, the whole atmosphere. It's my salvation. If things bother me, I'll go into my

room and lock the door, turn on my stereo, and escape
into my own world. I can just "space". Music is a lot
cheaper than drugs, and it's legal.

Music, of course, is always on the move, always experimenting with new sounds and mediums. Rock 'n' roll of
the 60s gave way to numerous variations of hard and soft
rock. The folk phenomenon was sandwiched in along the
way. The disco sound was popular, but short-lived. At the
moment, new wave is ruling the charts and spawning a
whole new lifestyle option. Before this book can be published and read, other innovative styles may well be moving
up the charts.

Although new wave and its electronic rhythmic wizardry
is sweeping the teen scene, rock is still a favourite of more
than three-quarters of the young people surveyed. Heavy
metal and new wave receive the applause of one in three,
while country and western gets high-level listening from
1 out of 5 teenagers. Classical, folk, and religious music at-
tract listening time from only about 1 out of 10 adolescents.

Music has often been the medium used by the younger
generation to hurl dissent at adult values and norms. In
the 1960s the folk ballad was the vehicle for anti-war proc-
lamations. The Beatles and other rock groups offered young
people their views on love and religion, drugs and sex, and
politics. Many younger people "bought in" and took their
heroes as models for hair length and personal lifestyles.

A cursory examination of the lyrics of popular songs
over the past several years leaves one with the impression
that the emphasis has tended to be on interpersonal relationships and feelings rather than on social issues.[12] There
is some evidence, however, that protest songs may be making a come-back. One Alberta university newspaper writer,
Zen Faulkes, has recently argued that since 1982 "more
acts than ever before are writing, recording and releasing
protest songs, although very few go under that name today."[13] He writes that these songs tend to focus on war and
nuclear issues. They include "It's a Mistake" by Men at

Work, "99 Luftballons" by Nena, Culture Club's "The War Song", "Two Tribes" by Frankie Goes to Hollywood, Ian Thomas's "Progress", "Look In Look Out" by Chilliwack, Platinum Blonde's "Standing in the Dark", and Bruce Cockburn's "If I Had a Rocket Launcher".

Today's most visible dissenters are probably the new wavers. Their roots lie in British punk rock and teenage culture. In their extreme form, new wavers have been labelled punkers. They are more than anti-establishment. They are anti-life. The prevailing themes of the punk subculture seem to revolve around the imagery of death, violence, perversion, loathsomeness, chaos, victimization, and the like.[14] They do not have an agenda for a better tomorrow. They simply are down on today.

Their strategy appears to be to shock the mainstream of society by being "repulsive". Their hair is spiked and dyed gaudy colours. Heads are partly or totally shaven. The punk dress code varies from totally ragged to basically dirty. Black jeans, black army boots, and black leather jackets are in vogue. Metal-studded leather belts around the waist, steel bullets circling the wrist, and chains hung about the neck complete the outfits. Milder new wavers dress in less ostentatious ways, including pegged pants, pedal pushers, and bobby socks.[15] Music is central to their milieu. They can be seen in any of our major cities.

Research consultant Steve Barnett suggests that new wave youth can be characterized by apathy about social issues, a sense of political powerlessness, a fascination with the creation of artificial environments, made possible by computer technology and electronic forms of music and communication, and a withdrawal into alternate worlds as a way of rebelling against a world in which they can have little significant involvement. Researchers Harold Levine and Steven Stumpf of the University of California at Los Angeles maintain that the appearance and themes of punkers involve two major functions: first, to generate an aura of intimidation aimed at insulating them from the dominant culture; and second, to reflect, through embodying the theme of fear in their dress and music, their perception of fear in the wider culture. "In short," they write, "the functional role of the punk subculture is to exist outside the main culture, while illuminating central features of it."[16]

Approximately 30% of Canadian teens frequently tune into their new wave music idols and respond to their high speed, frantic beats. This is not to say, of course, that many of the 30% are full-fledged new wavers themselves. The central core of the subculture is very small. Every movement obviously attracts a fringe element that never moves beyond the outer edge. Such is the status of most who appreciate new wave music or dye their hair "exotic" colours.

Moderate Sources of Happiness

Sports

About 45% of Canadian young people maintain that sports is a source of "a great deal" of enjoyment. Predictably, sports is particularly important to males (57% vs. 32% for females). Six in 10 males and 3 in 10 females say they follow sports, while about 3 in 10 of either sex are frequent attenders of sports events (see Table 3.2). Further, teenagers not only follow teams and stars. They are also active participants in both team and individual athletics. Some 1 in 3 young people play team sports (males 50%, females 29%) and participate in non-team activities (males 44%, females 37%). One-third also work out regularly (males 40%, females 35%).

These findings underline the major role competitive and non-competitive athletics play in the lives of Canadian adolescents, female as well as male. Given the involvement and interest of females, one cannot help but wonder why the media, out of self-interest if not in the interest of gender equality, have not employed more female sports announcers and sport writers. They may well be underestimating their healthy "female market".

A number of researchers have drawn attention to the importance of competitive athletic participation for teenage social esteem, especially for males.[17] In a society that places high value on physical attributes, and in an adolescent sub-society that is highly conscious of the emergence and non-emergence of those traits, the prestige accorded the male athlete is highly predictable. On the other hand, sex role socialization does not appear to lead to such automatic social enhancement for the female athlete. Athletic prowess in the sports world is seldom accorded parallel acclaim for males and females. Rather it is commonly seen as out of keeping with culturally desirable "feminine" traits, depending on the sports involved. Being a tennis, swimming, or golf star, for example is presumably associated with social approval for either sex. The same probably cannot be said for the female involved in sports such as track and field or basketball.

Television

Researchers tell us that Canadian preschool children typically watch television 20 hours a week and grade school children 22 hours. Sleeping, the researchers say, is the only activity that commands more of their time. By the age of eighteen, they will have spent more time in front of the TV set than anywhere else, including school.[18] Consequently, the role this medium plays in young lives has become a question of considerable importance.

The place of television in the lives of teenagers is intriguing. As a leisure activity choice, 57% of young people say they watch TV "very often". Yet only 29% indicate that they receive a "great deal" of satisfaction from their viewing.

TABLE 3.2   *Leisure Activities by Gender:*

"How often do you . . . ?"

		% Reporting "Very Often"	
	Nationally	*Males*	*Females*
Listen to music	90	89	92
Watch television	57	61	53
Daydream about the future	51	43	59
Sit and think	44	35	54
Dance	44	32	56
Attend parties	40	40	39
Follow sports	43	58	29
Participate in non-team sports	40	44	37
Play team sports	39	50	29
Work out	37	40	35
Attend a sports event	27	32	22
Read the newspaper	37	41	34
Follow the news	35	41	29
Spend time on a hobby	34	36	34
Read magazines	32	29	36
Read books	29	19	39
Participate in a youth group	17	14	19
Go to a movie	17	15	19
Go to a video games arcade	13	20	7
Play video games in a home	12	17	7

University of Chicago researchers Reed Larson and Robert Kubey[19] argue that television is something of an "alien" medium to teenagers. Programs are conceived and produced by older adults from the mainstream of society. Teenage characters appear only one-third as often as their actual numbers in the population. Furthermore, the television image of adolescents is often negative. In contrast, music is created and produced by individuals closer to the age of the teenagers themselves. Musicians tend to live on the fringes of society and are often at odds with accepted adult norms. Many teens readily identify with those "on the edge". And popular music speaks to central adolescent concerns, ranging from heterosexual relations to rebellion and autonomy. Music, therefore, becomes an essential ingredient in dating, parties, and dancing.

Furthermore, Larson and Kubey found that when teens watch TV, they often do so with family members or alone, but rarely with friends. On the other hand, when listening to music, they often were alone, one-quarter of the time were with friends, but virtually never were with adults. For many young people, then, television becomes an adult and family-related medium, whereas music is part of the teenage domain. The two researchers emphasize the expressive difference they found: "Music is much more successful in engaging youth in its world. When listening to music, adolescents reported greater emotional involvement. They reported higher motivation, greater excitement, and more openness. Watching television, in contrast, was associated with lower involvement. The adolescents reported feeling less motivated, more bored, and less free with this medium."[20]

Nevertheless, as with adults, television is used by many teenagers as a diversion from the problems of living, including loneliness and boredom. Four out of 10 teenagers told us that they frequently experience both. Television at least provides a different visual image, momentary removal, and sometimes necessary relief, from immediate reality. And as Saga points out, there may be little danger in escaping in such style, putting "our minds on idle" and letting "others take it for awhile".[21]

Psychologist Elkind offers the reminder that escape into different realities has its place in a society like ours. He notes that much of media content in recent years has been directed towards what he calls "the new realism", by which children and others have been made aware of the whole range of social ills. "Adolescents, no less than children," he writes, "need fantasy in order to deal with feelings and emotions which are not always clearly articulated."[22] He suggests that the real need is for creative writers who can produce quality material that challenges the imagination as well as entertains.

Thought and Reading

It is frequently stated that the omnipresence of the TV set, along with the pace of modern life, does not leave young people any time to think. Our survey findings show that at least some forms of thought are still alive and well. "Daydreaming about the future", along with sheer "sitting and thinking", are the third and fourth most common teenage activities, behind music listening and television viewing (see Table 3.2). In Styx's poetry, "I like daydreams, I've had enough reality."[23]

Considerable concern has also been expressed that television and our 70 mm visual world have created a generation of non-readers. We do not have data on past patterns but, currently, about 1 in 3 young people are involved in optional reading. This compares with 1 in 2 adults.[24] When it comes to both reading and thinking, teenage females surpass males.

York University sociologist Thelma McCormack makes the insightful observation that during adolescence interest in television and books declines while attention given movies, radio, records, and newspapers increases. "These," she says, "are media which can be enjoyed privately, which help to create mood, and strengthen peer group bonds . . . better than television does." McCormack's prophecies about television, written in 1979, have been fulfilled with the advent of cable music channels and specials along with the explosion of rock videos. She speculated that there might soon come a time when "multiple set ownership is widespread with teenagers having their own sets, and channel choices increased and specialized"; when "television may become more like present day radio with its disc jockeys and calculated appeals to the teenage market."[25]

That day has come. Not everyone is enthralled with its arrival. At the fall 1984 meeting of the Speech Communication Association in Chicago, several researchers reported that the "booming market of television music videos is crammed with bursts of sex and violence that reinforce stereotypes of women and minorities." In an interview, Barry Sherman, a professor of journalism at the University of Georgia, said, "If you're a non-white in video, you're there to blow someone up or to be blown up." Jane Brown of the University of North Carolina commented, "What I found most intriguing was that men are shown in social interactions — talking, dancing, whatever — getting a reaction. The female leads, on the other hand, look at other people but don't get responded to. So it's a real subtle kind of thing where the woman doesn't have as much power in a social relationship."[26]

Even superstar Michael Jackson fails to get an exemption from critics. Jackson, an active Jehovah's Witness, apologized to his fellow Witnesses in an 1984 interview in the church's magazine, *Awake*, acknowledging that his award-winning video "Thriller" had "offended a lot of people".[27]

Other Sources of Happiness

Some 1 in 3 teenagers report giving considerable time to *hobbies*, presumably involving a wide range of activities that are both private and social. Just under 1 in 5 say that they frequently attend movies. About 1 in 10 regularly play *video games*, either at an arcade (13%) or at home (12%), with males outnumbering females by almost 3 to 1 in both instances. Such video data attest to why video games and other computer hardware and software are big business in North America, accounting for $1.7-billion in U.S. sales in 1982. In that same year, one-game commercial machines alone brought in some $5-billion in revenue, with video-game machines paying for themselves in about six weeks.[28]

Approximately 20% of young people indicate that *cars* are an important source of enjoyment, including about 30% of males and 15% of females. The social and psychological significance of cars is well known. The car provides teenagers with a path to freedom from family and community. Adolescents spend hours in cars each day, eating in them, watching movies, talking with their friends, and, yes, making love.[29]

Psychologically, the car variously symbolizes power and excitement, masculinity and femininity, romance and sexuality. Advertisements, for example, imply that any male who drives a certain car will automatically fill it with beautiful females, or that any female who drives up in a certain car with plush upholstery will be considered glamorous and beautiful. Further, the car can also be a means of expressing hostility and anger, as a weapon to destroy, mutilate, and even kill. One youth culture expert writes, "The way adolescents use cars and the attitudes with which they drive are fair indications and tests of their emotional maturity."[30]

Part-time jobs, held by about 40% of the teens surveyed, are an important source of revenue and a valued diversion from other activities (see Table 3.1). Of those working, only 29% say they get "a great deal" of enjoyment from their jobs. Another 38% report "quite a bit" of enjoyment. These findings suggest that part-time work is psychologically gratifying for some, but a relatively unenjoyable means to a monetary end for many.

Limited Sources: School, Groups, and Religion

Of the seventeen areas and activities offered in the survey, the three at the bottom of the enjoyment list are school, youth groups, and church or synagogue life. Indeed, only about 1 in 5 say that they often participate in youth groups of any kind, while about 1 in 4 report that they often attend religious services. Only 1 in 10 claim to be personally involved in student union activities. A grade twelve male from a small town in southern Saskatchewan offers this opinion:

> Religion, hobby clubs, and other similar activities are not top priorities. People who are involved in one or more of these functions are usually considered losers.

The survey indicates that less than 2 in 10 highly enjoy school life. Another 4 in 10 claim "quite a bit" of gratification. The remaining half, however, find the whole experience to be less than inspiring. The church–synagogue predicament is even darker. Located at the very bottom of the gratification list at 8%, religious institutions nevertheless find that some 25% of teenagers are often in the pews. In part this apparent discrepancy is probably the product of parental pressure. It could also reflect an inculcated sense that "I need to be there, even though I don't particularly enjoy it."

It is important to keep in mind that even when teenagers do speak of experiencing enjoyment from institutional participation — here school and church life — this is not to say that their gratification comes primarily or even partially from the academic or religious components of either. Studies show that high-school students typically indicate that "relationships with other students" are "the best thing about school". They commonly exhibit a nonchalant or negative attitude towards academic matters, valuing instead the social dimension of school.[31] Yet even the best and most enthusiastic students express strong reservations about school. In the mid-1970s, an interesting poll of more than 22,000 students listed in *Who's Who Among High School Students* asked, "What do you think of the twelve years of education you have received?" Among the responses of these top students were the following:

39% said the time was challenging
50% said it was routine

54% said school was stimulating
37% said it was boring

55% said the teachers were good
38% said they were just adequate[32]

Perhaps even more seriously, evidence to date indicates that as young people move up through the grades, many become *decreasingly* interested in the academic program. With increasing age, enthusiasm seems to be "replaced by boredom and indifference, with school becoming a chore and a burden, punctuated by interest in sports events and holidays".[33] Mitchell argues that the reason for such apathy is not surprising: schools do not try to address the psychological needs of students who are in late adolescence; rather, they provide "an environment which is essentially early-adolescent in its scope and emphasis".[34] The schools, he maintains, act largely oblivious to such late-adolescent needs as self-worth and the importance of making a significant contribution.

A major problem is that school is mandatory and yet is perceived as only occasionally being either interesting or relevant to teenage concerns. Further, the school comes to symbolize restraint for freedom-minded young people. These kinds of perceptions are not unique to North America. A recent study of some 1,600 Australian adolescents found that they wanted their schools to be less authoritarian about rules and discipline. In addition, the students wanted to have more say in what they were taught. Finally, the Australian students felt teachers could be more friendly and caring.[35]

Assessment

For Canadian teenagers, the pre-eminent values of relational gratification and freedom find their primary fulfilment in friends and music. Parents, while a significant source of enjoyment for many, are less than a noteworthy happiness factor for a large number of young people.

As stated earlier, there is nothing wrong with young people supplementing healthy family ties with peer ties. There is, however, something amiss when companionship and love are highly valued, yet are infrequently found in relationships with adults.

Our findings point to the harsh possibility that for many a teenager friends and music are the major allies in the difficult transition into adulthood. Appropriately, another one of their own poets, The Human League, in their album, *Dare*, tells it straight: "Everyone needs two or three friends."[36]

Other important sources of gratification include sports, television, and — for those who have them — cars and jobs. School, youth organizations, and churches, on the other hand, are significant sources of enjoyment for relatively few.

The results are consistent with the reality of emergence. The lack of appreciation of young people for the school environment, youth groups, church life, and, for some, the family, offers a strong statement. One obvious message is that teenagers are not responding positively to structured settings that are often insensitive to their emergence. Many young people consequently quite unconsciously heed a sociological rule of thumb: groups insist on norms; therefore, one increases freedom by decreasing group ties. Teenagers accordingly abandon organized groups and churches. However, for most there still is school.

Some readers at this point might well be thinking, What on earth did those researchers expect? Since when did schools and churches become "fun" for kids, anyway? I never enjoyed them when I was their age. Why should they? We would reply that such a common response reflects a pro-adult, pro-institution position. For too long we have seen youth contact with parents, schools, churches, and the judicial system as inevitably negative experiences, as if somehow these things "are written in the stars". Some social scientists have even given scientific sanction to such a position. Kingsley Davis, an American sociologist prominent earlier in this century, once wrote that parent–youth conflict is virtually unavoidable as a result of factors including rapid social change, intergenerational conflict of norms, and the competition of other institutions, including the school and media.[37]

We disagree. As educator Dale Baughman has put it concerning school, "Youth is entitled to some joy, pleasure, and gaiety during school hours . . . There is no justification for denying that joy."[38] In taking for granted the folk wisdom that "school isn't fun," we forget a basic reality: most children are eager to begin school.[39] Yet somehow, somewhere along the way that enthusiasm is frequently lost. It need not be.

Likewise there is no inherent reason why young people should have to have unpleasant experiences with churches, the police, and parents, providing that those institutional "representatives" are sensitive to and respectful of teenage emergence. In contrast, it is our assertion that teenagers respond favourably to adults who recognize and facilitate their emergence.

Few people particularly covet conflict, or bask in boredom. People who morbidly think "That's just the way institutions are" will doom interaction before it begins. School personnel, curricula, and schedules in tune with the reality of emergence need not be inevitable recipients of hostility or apathy. Baughman, speaking specifically of schools, sums it up this way: "Secondary schools are for youth. Therefore, they should provide the kinds of experiences to help them to learn to live now and in the future as adults. It means further that schools can do a better job of treating students as adults and citizens . . . The secondary school must become more of an enabling institution . . ."[40]

Similarly, youth and religious organizations need not necessarily alienate teenagers, providing that they too are in touch with the requirements of emergence. In the words of the 1980 report of the United States National Commission on Youth: "Adolescents desire authoritative, but not authoritarian, adult relationships . . . The style in which [adults] present their views will determine the willingness of youth to respond. This precludes a 'when I was your age' approach."[41]

Dogmatic, paternalistic, and maternalistic styles — often associated with such organizations — are simply incompatible with the freedom young people crave to think for themselves, to act how they want to be and become. Individuals and groups that cannot accommodate such developments will simply be tolerated and, as soon as possible, ignored. An articulate sixteen-year-old female from Vancouver puts it this way:

> Most of the bad habits of teenagers arise from their wish to rebel against authority. If those in authority were less patronizing and more understanding, teenagers would probably not have as many bad habits. If adults will make an effort to understand teenagers more, perhaps then we can work together.

4

PERSONAL CONCERNS:

What Troubles Teenagers

Teens are expected to feel happy about themselves while enjoying their "carefree" years. These years I find are hard, trying, and painful—it's basically growing up and coming to terms with the fact that you're now almost an adult and can't depend on anyone.

— a sixteen-year-old female from Ontario

The Myth of "The Trouble-Free Years"

It is common for adults to look at the teen years as "the fun years", a time characterized by satisfaction and security, freedom and frivolity. The teen years, they believe, provide a comfortable prelude to the time when one must settle down, take life seriously, and assume responsibility. Many a parent has quipped, "Why shouldn't teenagers be happy? What have they got to worry about?"

Such observations may make sense from an adult's point of view. But how soon we forget. The movement into adulthood involves far more than merely "getting older" and "growing up". Those things are easy. The difficulty lies in the complex nature of teenage emergence, each facet of which carries with it considerable importance. Teenagers have a lot to worry about — and they do worry.

The demands of emergence? Psychologist Robert Havighurst has maintained that adolescents have eight "developmental tasks" to carry out in order to function as mature people:

1. Accepting one's physique and using the body effectively.
2. Achieving new and more mature relations with age mates of both sexes.
3. Achieving a masculine or feminine sex role.
4. Achieving emotional independence from parents and other adults.
5. Preparing for an economic career.
6. Preparing for marriage and family life.
7. Desiring and achieving socially responsible behavior.
8. Acquiring a set of values and an ethical system as a guide to behavior.[1]

Physically, young people are saying goodbye to childhood. Puberty comes earlier than it did a century ago. The average North American girl has her first menstrual period at 12.5 years today, compared with 14.2 in 1900; boys' puberty, marked by sperm production, is complete at an average age of fourteen.[2]

Depending on the information available to them, teenagers commonly report bewilderment and anxiety concerning the beginning of menstruation or the first nocturnal emission ("wet dream").[3] The experience of this sixteen-year-old American is probably typical: "I was very frightened of the sexual changes that occurred in my body. The first change I noticed was my menstrual period. I was very frightened of the blood; I didn't know why it occurred. When I finally asked my mother, she did not really take the time to explain to me, so I didn't really know just why or how it happened."[4] Alfred Kinsey found adolescent males to be both confused and guilty over nocturnal emissions. One mother accused her son of wetting the bed, obviously making him feel childish and embarrassed in the process.[5]

But the physical changes have more than immediate biological consequences. Young people find that a particular kind of physical being is emerging, one that is critically graded by a highly physically conscious society that tends to reward the physically attractive with social, occupational, and service privileges, to name just a few. On the other side of the coin, the unattractive find themselves in a disadvantaged position.

The growing body of research on this topic has yielded highly consistent results. Unattractive people are seen as less intelligent, less popular, less happy, less likely to continue their education, less likely to obtain prestigious jobs, more dishonest and unkind, more aggressive and anti-social. What is even more serious, the evidence suggests that people act on these stereotypes. The unattractive are liked less, their work is more likely to be judged inferior, and their problems are more likely to be blamed on their alleged anti-social condition.[6]

While accomplishments may in time to some extent override such physical yardsticks, especially for men,[7] they are too far removed from the teen years to provide much immediate compensation. Not being at least reasonably attractive is a teenage tragedy.

The sheer rate of change during puberty can create problems. Early maturers and late maturers who are "out of step" with their peers experience considerable strain. It is no blessing to be "too" tall or short, "too" big or small, "too" developed or underdeveloped.[8] One struggles "to fit in", gaining little consolation from waiting for the others to catch up, or wondering if one will ever catch up.

And then there is the problem of what to wear. Researchers have documented what most of us have suspected or experienced. Clothing is a central component of teenage acceptance. Adolescents who are "sharp dressers" have high status.[9] But in the teenage world, being a sharp dresser is not merely to be functionally well-attired. One has to wear "the right" clothes. For some, running shoes and jeans have to bear just the right manufacturer's label. Jeans have to be faded just so. For others, their father's old sweater, trousers a size or two too short, and army boots complete the proper ensemble. Keeping in mind just what "fashionable" means in this context, it is interesting to note one American researcher's finding that teens defined by their peers as fashionable dressers have high status; the well-dressed but not fashionable students have moderate status; and the poorly dressed students have the lowest status.[10]

Given such a multitude of factors influencing physical appearance and its centrality to one's sense of self, it is hardly surprising that teenagers are commonly observed to be highly "self-conscious". Yet it would be extremely naive to equate adolescents' concern about appearance with self-centredness. Many teenagers are anxious and frightened performers on the social stage, barely "hanging in there" as they wait for others to tell them "what they look like".

Socially, teenagers are increasingly having to learn how to relate to the adult world and, of course, to the opposite sex. This includes becoming adept verbally and behaviourally. In general, teens are supposed to be "maturing". Both adults and peers admonish them to "act their age". But the rules are not always the same. Adults expect them to act older than they are but often seem to treat them as if they were younger. And their peers ridicule them if they act either younger *or* older than they are.

It is not an easy normative high wire to walk, especially when a person is around adults and peers at the same time. It can be a strain to talk to a teacher or a parent with friends looking on. It can also be difficult to talk to one's friends when an adult is in the vicinity. A teenager almost needs to be able to speak two dialects and have two different sets of behaviour. Sometimes it is not even socially safe for the one to be seen in the other's presence.

Intellectually, most young people find that the more they learn, the more complicated the world seems to get. Life somehow seemed so much simpler a few years before. Then there is the question of what life itself is all about. Here the immediate identity question of "Who am I?" is supplemented by the larger identity question of "Why am I?"[11] Is there a purpose to life or do we have to create one? A grade eleven Vancouver student comments:

> It is difficult at times to decide between one thing and another. There are so many in-betweens in my life, so many questions about world events, personal events, life and death. I do not think these questions are unnatural, indeed they are part of "growing up", and I do not expect them to be answered by the time I'm 30.

According to psychologists such as Jean Piaget, the apparent increasing complexity of the world for teenagers is no accident. Mental development, they maintain, involves a number of stages. The adolescent years are characterized by the newly-found ability to think abstractly, to systematize ideas and deal critically with them ("the formal operational stage").[12] This cognitive development makes it possible for "young people to think about thinking".[13] They experience new levels of self-consciousness and an enhanced ability to reason. Their increased capacity to think reflectively makes it possible for them to evaluate what they have been taught. It enables them to discern not only what the adult world is but also what it could be. The increasing ability to reflect also gives teenagers the potential to become idealistic rebels.[14]

Sexually, the equipment is assembled and the curiosity is intense. There are lots of questions and lots of feelings. But adolescents find that it is often difficult to locate people to whom they can safely talk. Most parents and other adults do not seem to be aware of what is happening and would probably be upset if they found out. Even one's friends seem to know more, and have either "done more" or "done less" — so it is not always helpful to talk to them. (Teenagers' feelings about physical intimacy will be examined in the next chapter.)

Psychologically, their identity or sense of who they are is being dramatically overhauled in the light of their physical, social, intellectual, and sexual changes. Renowned psychologist Erik Erikson sees adolescence as perhaps the most pronounced period of identity crisis in anyone's life. He maintains that seven conflicts have to be resolved by young people in the course of their finding firm identities: developing a sense of time; self-confidence; experimenting with various roles; exploring vocational possibilities; gender identification; personal and social allegiances; commitment to values. According to Erikson, failure to resolve these conflicts by young adulthood results in the lack of a clear-cut identity, or what he calls role and identity "diffusion".[15]

Financially, emergence costs money. One's appearance, social life, and personal possessions do not come cheaply. The anxiety about money is heightened considerably by the fact that most teenagers are highly dependent financially on their parents. These, of course, are the same parents who, in many instances, are not particularly sensitive to the problems associated with their emergence experience.

Vocationally, the time is getting short. A major question is the future — what to be, what to do. On the surface, at least, our highly specialized society besieges young people with career choices. One observer tells us that *The Dictionary of Occupational Titles* now lists almost 50,000 different occupations.[16] As if this were not confusing enough, there is also the pressure imposed by adults, especially parents.

In sum, the teenage years represent a time of considerable stress brought on by the multidimensional nature of their emergence. Life for adolescents is far more than merely "fun and games". In the words of one fifteen-year-old rural Ontario male:

> I think being a teenager today is a lot tougher than it was for our parents.

The Canadian Picture

Life Beyond Graduation

The major personal concern of Canadian young people — characterizing almost 70% of them — is what they are going to do when they finish school (see Table 4.1). Such anxiety about the future is pervasive throughout Canada's five regions and is equally felt by females (71%) and males (67%). A seventeen-year-old Albertan states the problem succinctly:

> Young people of today are at a cross-roads faced with many uncertainties. These include the future of Canada, the world, and they themselves.

For some that anxiety is intensified by current economic conditions. The "tough economic times" of the mid-1980s have left more than one million Canadians looking for work, with almost half of these between the ages of fifteen and twenty-four. A July 1984 issue of *Maclean's* magazine focused on youth unemployment, calling it "one of the most potentially dangerous social problems that Canada has had to face since the depression of the 1930s".[17] Even being unable to find part-time or temporary work is a source of anxiety for many. One grade twelve male student in a small northern Alberta community says:

> My major problem is what to do after I graduate. If I can't get a summer job, I can't go to college, and my plans will be ruined. I need a job and there aren't many jobs to be found.

For most, decisions concerning the years immediately after high school involve a variety of interacting variables. They include ultimate vocation, education, travel, moving out, moving away, and marriage.

Finances

Money ranks second on the concern list of teenagers. Some 54% are troubled in a major way by money matters, exactly the same proportion as for adults.[18] For both teenagers and adults in our affluent society, dollar concerns pertain not so much to "staying alive" as they do to "living well".[19]

Merchandisers carefully target the youth sector in creating a demand for their products. The power of youth peer pressure is carefully tapped by advertising firms. The effectiveness of such marketing and promotion is there to be seen. Designer jeans with the proper label on the back pocket can become a life and death issue. Recreational shoes are carefully selected from display walls featuring 60 different variations — and only two or three "acceptable" manufacturers' names.

As noted earlier, some 40% of teenagers have part-time jobs, but almost half of these jobs involve ten hours of work a week or less. Revenue from job sources, therefore, is frequently modest. About three-quarters of Canada's teens are very dependent on their parents for money. Indeed, about 50% receive allowances. Of these on "the weekly dole", 25% receive $5 or less, about 40% get $6 to $10, and another 25% pocket $11 to $25. The remaining 10% constitute "the affluent minority", getting allowances of more than $25 a week.

Because of this partial to total financial dependence of young people on parents, money and commodities, such as a car, can become poignant symbols of teen–parent tension. Dependent sons and daughters can perceive their freedom and self-respect eroded drastically by adults who use resources as a means of controlling them. Things are not made easier by the tendency of young people to think parents have money but are reluctant to share it. About 90% feel that their family's income is average or above; only about 75% of adults share the same sentiments.[20]

Here the power relationship is not dissimilar to that between employee and employer. One major difference on the positive side is that it is more durable, because of the family bond. A major difference on the negative side is that it can be more intolerable, because it is largely involuntary.

Consequently there is a direct correlation between the amount of money teenagers *control* and the level of freedom and independence they can express. In our society, we are not regarded as autonomous adults until we are completely self-supporting. Money becomes one of the necessary keys to unlock the door of the adult world.

School

Some 50% of teenagers say that they are bothered "a great deal" or "quite a bit" by school. As we saw in Chapter Three, it is not just that school is often not a source of enjoyment. School also produces considerable stress and anxiety. Students are pressured by society not only to perform but also to excel. Many clearly are "feeling under the gun", some just to pass and others to meet higher expectations. That superstar of the cartoon strips, Charlie Brown, summed it up about as well as anyone: "There's no heavier burden than a great potential."[21]

As a result of this pressure, students, probably no less and perhaps more than adults, commonly have to "bring their work home with them". Almost 50% say that they very often do homework, while a further 40% have to sometimes. Less than 5% never do homework.

We may safely say that a certain proportion of students are performing well and are not troubled by school, and that 1 in 2 are experiencing a high level of strain. The

TABLE 4.1   *Personal Concerns by Region:*

"How often do these common problems bother you?"

% Reporting "A Great Deal" or "Quite a Bit"

	Nationally	B.C.	Prairies	Ontario	Quebec	Atlantic
What I am going to do when I finish school	68	70	68	64	70	72
Money	54	56	56	54	53	55
School	50	57	49	51	47	51
Time	48	49	45	48	51	47
My looks	44	41	40	42	52	43
Wondering about the purpose of life	44	41	44	40	52	44
Boredom	43	45	43	41	43	46
My height or weight	43	45	45	45	38	47
Loneliness	35	33	33	33	40	38
Feeling that I am not as good as others	29	36	27	28	28	26
Sex	28	26	29	26	29	29
My parents' marriage	20	21	19	20	21	22

stereotype that many teenagers are simply taking up seats and putting in time should therefore receive little support. Students may not particularly enjoy school, but it is nonetheless their ticket to peace with parents and future employment. It is evident that many do not take the ticket for granted.

There are, of course, other areas of strain at school beyond the academic sphere. As the locus for a good portion of a teenager's life, the school can be unpleasant because of problems and conflict with teachers and peers. The ending of romantic relationships, interpersonal tension, intimidation, violence, and theft are just some areas of school life that can present problems for adolescents.

Time

Five in 10 teenagers also say that they never seem to have enough time; more than 6 in 10 adults say the same thing.[22] Yet, interestingly, almost an equal proportion of adolescents say that boredom is a serious problem for them, including 50% of those who allegedly have insufficient time.

Clearly, like the rest of us, teenagers have things to do that exceed the time available. But this is not to say that the activities are all enjoyable, purposeful, or exciting. Like us, many teenagers are frequently bored by the things they do. For a considerable number of adults, boredom is related to work. For many students, it is associated with school.

Appearance

As would be expected, a high proportion of Canadian teenagers — just under 1 in 2 — admit that their physical appearance concerns them considerably. While teens are well aware that dramatic physical changes are taking place, they also know that little can be done to influence the outcome — "one gets what one gets." For a number of years the drama continues, keeping young people in unnerving suspense. They are like children opening Christmas presents, knowing that the outcome of the maturing process can bring happiness or disappointment, relief or anxiety. Bruce Springsteen puts the pain to music: looking into the mirror, many a teen concludes, "I wanna change my clothes, my hair, my face."[23] They smile and moan privately, and compare notes collectively. A young Saskatoon woman of seventeen states the problem bluntly:

> This is a very hard time. We have recently gone through puberty and are trying to find acceptance of our new selves.

The extent to which teenagers will go to alter their physical appearances can be seen in their consumption of an endless variety of cosmetics and beauty aids, as well as clothing that can enhance their looks. Dieting, sometimes to a detrimental extreme, is also common, particularly among females.

One pathological extreme is anorexia nervosa, the severe psychological condition in which the pursuit of elusive thinness leads to starving oneself. The result, as in the highly publicized case of popular music star Karen Carpenter, can be death. Anorexia nervosa in 95% of the cases involves females. It is estimated that this is a characteristic of between 1 in 100 and 1 in 250 adolescent girls.[24] The most common age for the onset of anorexia nervosa is fourteen to fifteen. Anorexics are typically highly intelligent, good students, reserved, over-sensitive, conscientious, meticulous, and have an exaggerated sense of duty.

Medical experts, after three centuries of study, are still debating the causes and proper treatment of anorexia nervosa. There does, however, appear to be agreement on its symptoms. Dr. Joseph Silverman, a professor of pediatrics in New York, says that "any girl who has lost weight and has missed a number of periods should be considered anorexic."[26] Florida researcher Felicia Romeo has argued in a recent article that anorexia is related to anxiety about sexual development. Some girls, she says, are overwhelmed by their bodily changes, menstruation, breast development, and emerging sexuality. They therefore diet and, through self-starvation, alter their physical appearance to childlike proportions.[27]

What has been described as one of the latest "dieting epidemics" is a slightly different condition that has been labelled "bulimia". Here individuals go through periods of binge-eating alternating with purging through self-induced vomiting or the use of laxatives. Estimates of its incidence among young people have ranged from 2% to 13%.[28] Central to this condition seems to be the feeling that one has failed to meet one's own expectations and the expectations of others.[29]

The problem of obesity should also not be minimized. It has been estimated that 10% to 15% of adolescents are obese, with the problem more common among females than males.[30] Overweight teenagers may have a number of social and psychological problems. These include being stigmatized by peers, low self-esteem, poor adjustment to sexual development, over-dependency on parents, and academic difficulties caused by personal problems.[31] Further, being overweight as a teenager is not just a temporary phenomenon. About 80% of obese teenagers continue to be overweight as adults.[32]

Finally, for some teenagers, the problem is not excessive weight but insufficient weight. There is little joy in finding oneself skinny. Research reveals that, as with being overweight, being underweight has its social and psychological costs. One study has found that even teachers are not exempt from stereotyping, associating skinny students with a lack of both physical and social skills.[33]

The Gender Factor. Although the feminist movement has exhorted women to find their value and identity apart from their appeal to men, this country's female teenagers — consistent with the findings on anorexia — give evidence of being disproportionately preoccupied with their physical appearance. Young females (56%) are far more inclined than males (31%) to acknowledge concern about *their height and weight* specifically, and their *looks* more generally (52% vs. 38%).

Perhaps we should not find this surprising. Despite the apparent "feminist purge" of the 1970s, including the establishment of the Royal Commission on the Status of Women, our major institutions continue to perpetuate sexist stereotypes. Teenage women are frequently subjected to double messages. On the one hand, feminists pressing for equality and dignity are featured on the six o'clock news. Yet two hours later, the same television network slots the "Miss Universe" contest in prime time. Commercials may feature a woman with a Ph.D. carefully examining the oranges used in the family orange juice, but she is still making the breakfast.[34] Situation comedies continue to stereotype female sex appeal as every woman's greatest virtue. Many rock videos send the same message. The results show up in our data.

A 1978 study carried out for the Advisory Council on the Status of Women by Alice Courtney and Thomas Whipple noted that many Canadian television ads show a woman as:

- begging the male announcer not to take away her bleach
- being a hapless housewife who is flustered to learn from the male announcer that her peanut butter or detergent of ten years is inferior to the advertised brand
- having her self-confidence shattered by spotty drinking glasses
- feeling more like a woman because she is wearing the right bra[35]

There are signs that things may be improving. Reporting on the treatment of female characters in the 1984 television season, the U.S. National Commission on Working Women acknowledged that television is "doing better". Programs, it says, are getting away from the past pattern when "the prevailing picture of female TV characters was young, white, single, beautiful women". Men, "instead of being locked into aggressive roles, actually care for their children and love their families, without being objects of ridicule". The commission noted that ten years ago, men outnumbered women in TV roles 3 to 1, but that in the 1984 season 67 of the 143 new TV characters were women. Further, 76% of adult female TV characters in new shows have jobs outside the home, compared with 60% of actual American women.

The commission pointed out that some stereotypes remain. Females still tend to be young and beautiful, with the "female as victim" theme still prevalent. Citing the program *Mike Hammer*, it commented that "beautiful women get killed each week and the only continuing female character is the curvaceous secretary, Velda, who comes to work in extremely tight, low-cut dresses."[36] A seventeen-year-old from northern Alberta gives this related view:

> Men and women should be treated according to how well they do their jobs, not [according to] their sex.

A society like ours, which increasingly offers females and males a variety of sex-role possibilities, makes the resolution of the adolescent sex-role identity problem more difficult than in societies in which everyone knows what it means to be a man or a woman. Adult models may be providing so many different roles that adolescent choices are too varied for easy sex-role acceptance. While this is not necessarily a negative trend, having to make such choices increases the pressure on adolescents who already have many questions about sex-role identity.[37]

Purpose

It is noteworthy that in the midst of these concerns with immediate issues — the future, money, school, time, and physical appearance — more than 40% of teenagers across the country say they give considerable thought to the question of the purpose of life. Concern with so-called everyday issues does not appear to negate concern for "what it all means". One fifteen-year-old Calgarian puts it this way:

> I often wonder what our purpose in life is because it seems like such a waste to me that we live for 70–80 years and then die.

While teenagers are not particularly enchanted with religious organizations, that is not to say that their emergence lacks a serious spiritual component. One young Ontario woman seems to capture the feelings of many young people when she notes:

> I don't believe that in order to be near or "accepted" by God that you have to be in church.

Only 10% may highly enjoy church life, but *another* 35% highly value acceptance by God. Beyond both of these categories, still *another* 25% are concerned about resolving the question of the purpose of life. Thus, some 70% of teenagers seemingly have clear religious and spiritual interests. To the extent that religious groups fail to captivate young people, it is not because "the religious market" is not an appreciable one.

Loneliness

Anne Frank commented in her famous *Diary*, "In its innermost depths, youth is lonelier than old age."[38] The national survey has revealed that 35% of Canadian teenagers are deeply bothered by loneliness — an alarming finding considering the value they place on relationships. Nationally, the figure for adults, 31%, is slightly lower.[39] By gender, teenage females report a slightly *higher* level of loneliness than males.

It would appear that, in many instances, while friendships provide more gratification than family life in addressing the need for companionship and love, they also often fall short of offering fulfilment. The complex and diverse nature of emergence makes it difficult for any one friend or any one adult to provide understanding and help along *all* of its dimensions. Not infrequently, there is also the perception that people "don't care". A Moncton, New Brunswick female in grade twelve comments:

> I find being a teenager quite difficult. The hardest thing for me is trying to stay happy. The more I get to know people, the more I can't stand their coldness. There seems to be little warmth and a large lack of understanding — should be vice-versa.

As a result, teenagers frequently feel they have to "go it alone", not because — as with solitude — they choose to, but simply because there is no alternative.

In such moments, as in the more pleasurable ones, the role of music should not be underestimated. It undoubtedly functions as an invaluable "companion" for many. One American study documented that teenagers frequently draw on music in coping with anger and hurt.[40] Elton John, in his song "Sad Songs Say So Much", writes that such songs "reach into your room, just feel their gentle touch".[41]

Self-Image

The stereotype that teenagers are more cocky than adults is not borne out by the survey. Feelings of inferiority appear to be a major cause for concern for about 1 in 3 teens, compared with only 1 in 4 in the case of adults.[42] Teenage females (35%) are somewhat more likely than males (23%) to admit to having such feelings. More specifically, the survey has found that the overwhelming majority of teens tend to see themselves as being as nice looking or as well liked as most people (see Table 4.2). As for conversational confidence, more than half say they are comfortable among

TABLE 4.2   *Self-Image*

"Please indicate how accurately the following statements describe you."

% *Reporting "Very Well" or "Fairly Well"*

	Nationally	Males	Females
"I'm as nice looking as most people"	88	89	87
"I'm as well-liked as most people"	84	85	83
"I'm comfortable introducing myself to people I don't know"	60	58	62
"I find it easy to speak out in class"	59	63	55

strangers or in a classroom setting. Slightly more males than females tend to claim confidence in the classroom situation.

It should be emphasized that the self-image of teenagers who are "creatively different" as well as "destructively different" is under tremendous assault by adults who are excessively oriented towards conventional norms. Teenagers who "march" to the proverbial "different drummer" are commonly either broken and applauded on the one hand, or rebel and are stigmatized on the other. This latter response to conventional adults is expressed well by the rock group, Quiet Riot. In their song "Metal Health", they sing of the young person who is told he has "no brains" by a mother who can't control him and that he is "one big pain" by a teacher who calls him out of step with the times. The youth protests that he is not a loser, that he is "frustrated, not outdated", adding, "I really wanna be overrated."[43]

Sexuality and Family Life

Many teenagers also express concern about sexuality and their parents' marriage. In the next two chapters we will look at these two areas in detail.

Assessment

The bewildering nature of emergence makes it a difficult experience to handle alone. The survey results indicate that the majority of teenagers *do* receive the necessary understanding and help from their peers and, to a lesser extent, from adults. In the words of one young female from a small Ontario town:

> In many cases parents and adults do not understand kids today. I'm glad to say my parents are not like this.

But as she indicates, a sizeable minority of teenagers are finding the experience difficult, in large part because such sensitivity, assistance, and encouragement is inadequate. As Def Leppard asks in its music, "Is anybody out there? Anybody care?"[44]

This leads us to a highly related phenomenon: suicide. Psychologist Erikson has written that adolescents who fail to gain a sense of identity and adequate self-worth withdraw from reality, perhaps even from life.[45] Teenage suicide is being viewed as a problem of increasing proportions in both Canada and the U.S. Precise numbers are difficult to determine both because of social stigma and the problem of discerning when a death is through suicide. Official records for 1982, however, indicate that some 1,300 Canadian teenagers took their lives. Further, some estimates project between 30 and 100 attempts for every "successful" suicide. Toronto psychiatrist Barry Garfinkel, who has studied the problem extensively, says, "Teenage suicide and attempted suicide has escalated 300% in North America during the past thirty years and is continuing to climb, making it the fastest-increasing fatal medical problem."[46] University of Lethbridge sociologist Menno Boldt, who headed the Alberta Task Force on Suicide, writes that suicide is the second leading cause of death, behind accidents, for young people aged fifteen to twenty-four. He stresses that "suicide, particularly among youth, is a serious social and health problem."[47]

The extensive literature on suicide has documented some patterns.[48] Female teenagers are more likely than males to attempt suicide, but males — primarily because they use more violent means — are more likely than females to actually kill themselves.

Suicidal adolescents tend to come from homes characterized by emotional turmoil and strain. Further, they commonly have a sense of isolation, both socially and emotionally. Indeed, psychologists Yacoubian and Lourie go so far as to say that "social isolation appears to be the most effective factor in distinguishing those who kill themselves from those who will not."[50] Depression and stress are seen as the key immediate precipitating factors.

A disturbing finding reported by Joseph Teicher is that 40% of the adolescents he studied who attempted suicide had a family member or close friend who had committed suicide.[51] This observation suggests that suicide is literally "a learned option" for some young people. Equally disturbing is the important finding of Boldt concerning intergenerational attitudes towards suicide. In an examination of grade twelve students and their parents in Calgary, Boldt found young people to be more tolerant of suicide and less fearful of its consequences than their parents. Hence, he writes, "in a crisis, the act is more 'available' to them than it is to the parental generation." He concludes that if positive incentives to continue living are not provided, "these new values may predispose a society toward higher suicide rates."[52]

Teenagers certainly do not downplay the suicide issue. Asked "How serious do you think the problem of teenage suicide is in Canada?", more than 70% responded "very serious" or "fairly serious". Only 4% felt teenage suicide is "not a problem" at all. Young people ranked the matter of their friends or themselves taking their lives close to the threat of nuclear warfare and saw it as a more important issue than divorce. Significantly, more females than males perceived the problem to be extremely serious (47% vs. 31%). One young woman from Ontario confided:

> I was really angry at God. I blamed him for the suicide
> of a really close friend of mine in January. I was also
> angry that he wouldn't let me die when I tried suicide
> in February. I've gotten my head together since then
> and I guess there's a reason I'm still alive.

Contrary to widely-held opinion, suicide attempts in a great majority of cases are considered in advance and weighed against available alternatives.[53] Boldt reports that biographies of suicide victims reveal pre-death events pointing to suicide in more than 90% of cases. These pre-death events include threats, previous attempts, and abrupt changes in outlook (depression or sudden improvement). However, these clues typically go unnoticed or unheeded. He emphasizes that informed recognition and response to such pre-suicidal clues on the part of the public and professionals would likely reduce suicide rates.[54]

American psychiatrist Boris Zoubok is in agreement. In a late 1984 appearance on *Good Morning America*, Zoubok summed up the need for recognition and response this way: "One has to be there, one has to look, and one has to listen."[55]

There also is a need to encourage adolescents to turn to available help. According to Diane Syer-Solursh of Toronto East General Hospital's Crisis Intervention Unit, one factor in young males' taking their lives more than females is the culturally instilled idea that "boys are supposed to learn how to cope alone, to be a man and not cry."[56]

Adults, along with teenage friends, are consequently left with the significant task of being sensitive to such troubled young people. If ever some teenagers did not need parental and teacher, medical and religious "opponents", these are they. Their appearance and their words cannot be allowed to disguise them. Today's teenagers are struggling.

5

SEXUALITY

How Teenagers Feel About Physical Intimacy

Today, sex amongst teens before marriage is an everyday occurrence, whether love is involved or not.

—a seventeen-year-old female from Nova Scotia

Sexual Change and Stability

Teenagers are intrigued with sex. Their physical development, coupled with their social development, makes the sexual sphere biologically and socially alluring and exciting. Unlike adults, however, adolescents are not as preoccupied with the sexual quest as with the need to understand their emerging sexuality and to know what to do with it.[1] Coping with this dimension of emergence is far from easy.

After virtually centuries of being hidden in bedrooms, sexuality has been increasingly liberated *as a topic for discussion*. Sex has become a common conversational item. In open, explicit form it has found its way into the print, sound, and sight media. In its wide-ranging manifestations, sexuality is available through magazines, books, newspapers, movies, records, and videos. It is no longer a stranger to school and church curricula. Advertising cherishes it.

Our culture has seemingly become a little more European. Adults on the Continent took sexuality as a normal part of life, not to be flaunted in front of children but not to be hidden either. "Much as children in Europe were allowed to have a little wine," says Elkind, "they were exposed to some facets of sexuality as a preparation for adulthood."[2] Adults are also well aware that sex, besides "being out there for the taking", is now under control, thanks to the birth-control contributions of modern technology. Such "advances", of course, have not been welcomed by all. The availability of birth-control devices, for example, has had a well-known divisive effect on the Roman Catholic Church. In the words of one writer, "Almost as a symbol of the technological age, the modern-day Martin Luther of the Catholic Church is a birth-control pill."[3] Another technological donation, the automobile, has further offered teenagers unprecedented freedom of space and movement.

Factors such as these have led many observers to assert that "a sexual revolution" has been taking place. The overt sexuality of the post-1950s in its various heterosexual, homosexual, group, and promiscuous forms, the alleged increase in pornography, and the increase in the openness and frequency of abortion — taken together these seemingly confirm the existence of the revolution for many.

Yet, accepting the inclination of our institutions to instil in adolescents adult values and norms, it is difficult to envision that a "sexual revolution" could take place almost overnight. There is obviously a big difference between noting that groupings within the population are departing from widely held norms and asserting that such departures characterize the population as a whole. Keeping in mind the penchant of the media to "dabble in deviance" in response to our intrigue with "forbidden difference", we should hardly have to be cautioned about generalizing from "who makes news" to the general populace.

Now we are hearing that North Americans are "swinging back to the right", sexually and otherwise. What is not at all clear is whether we ever, as a population, had swung very far to the left. Sociologist Rodney Stark has noted that in the case of homosexuality, what seemingly increased in the 1960s and 1970s was "not its frequency but its visibility".[4] There is good reason to believe that, apart from some long-term changes in a more permissive direction for premarital sex and abortion, Stark's observation may hold for sexual attitudes and behaviour generally.

The Canadian Teenage Sex Scene

The importance of sex among Canadian teenagers can be seen in the survey findings. Four in 10 admit that they think about sex "very often", while about 3 in 10 acknowledge that it is an area that concerns them "a great deal" or "quite a bit". Further, 95% point out that sex is a theme that is "very often" (70%) or "sometimes" (25%) the subject of the jokes told by the people they know.

Sexual Relations

We asked our sample specifically about appropriate physical behaviour on dates involving people who *like* each other. Some 90% say that it is all right to *hold hands* on the first date; less than 1% feel it wrong after a few dates (see Table 5.1). *Kissing* is seen as appropriate on the first date by 82%, after a few dates by another 18%. *Necking* is acceptable on the first date, say 50%, while an additional 45% feel it is okay after a few dates. *Petting* — physical involvement from the neck down — is viewed as all right on the first date by 28% and after a few dates by a further 56% and a total of 84%.

Eleven percent of the teenage population endorse having *sexual relations* on the first date. Another 42%, for a

TABLE 5.1   *Appropriate Behaviour on Dates by Gender and Religion (In %'s)*

"If two people on a date like each other, do you think it is all right for them to:"

	Nationally	Males	Females	Prot.	R.C.	None
Hold Hands						
Yes, first date	92	92	91	95	90	93
Yes, after a few dates	8	7	9	5	10	6
No	0	1	0	0	0	1
Kiss						
Yes, first date	82	84	80	85	79	85
Yes, after a few dates	18	16	19	15	20	15
No	0	0	1	0	1	0
Neck						
Yes, first date	50	59	42	50	49	55
Yes, after a few dates	45	38	52	47	45	41
No	5	3	6	3	6	4
Pet						
Yes, first date	28	42	16	22	31	31
Yes, after a few dates	56	50	63	58	57	55
No	15	8	20	19	12	13
Love each other (write-in)	1	—	1	1	—	1
Have Sexual Relations						
Yes, first date	11	19	3	9	10	16
Yes, after a few dates	42	51	33	36	43	53
No	44	29	59	51	44	29
Love each other (write-in)	3	1	5	4	3	2

total of *half of Canada's teenagers*, feel that intercourse is appropriate after a few dates.

In short, when the couple like each other, more than 9 in 10 Canadian teenagers view holding hands, kissing, and necking as acceptable within a few dates. Eight in 10 feel the same about petting. Five in 10 feel the same about sexual relations.

Further, while the survey has found that 80% of the country's young people hold that premarital sex is all right when people *love* each other, more than 50% feel relations are also acceptable within a few dates when individuals *like* each other.

Given the transient nature of teenage romance, the possible behavioural implications of such sexual attitudes are somewhat staggering. And, indeed, these attitudes do not appear to be dissociated from behaviour. A variety of North American studies indicate that approximately 50% of fifteen- to nineteen-year-olds have premarital intercourse, with the range running from about 33% for fifteen-year-olds to 67% for nineteen-year-olds.[5] A recent publication, *Sexual Behaviour of Canadian Young People* by Edward S. Herold of the family studies department, University of Guelph, quotes one person's evolving views on premarital sex.

> At age 15 I believed: "I'll never have sex until marriage."
> At age 18 I believed: "If you are in love then sex is okay."
> At age 21 I believed: "If you are both in the mood, then why not?"[6]

For their part, teenagers don't act overly surprised. One Alberta sixteen-year-old quips:

> This is 1984, wake up mom! Everyone has sexual relations.

An Ontario student, a grade eleven female, is somewhat philosophical and fatalistic about it all:

> I think that too much emphasis is put on sex for teen-
> agers. So what if someone goes to bed with someone
> else. It's their lives and it doesn't have to be the talk of
> the town. If adults do that, then it is no big deal, but as
> soon as teenagers "do it" it's a crime.

The title of one of Olivia Newton-John's hit songs —
"Let's Get Physical" — seems to sum up the teenage sentiment succinctly. Speaking for "girls", Cyndi Lauper, in
her album *She's So Unusual*, tells us "girls just want to
have fun."[7] Speaking for the boys, Huey Lewis and the
News reply that if she takes "her chances with me", then
"she gets what she wants."[8]

Regarding "necking onward" there are some interesting
variations by gender and religious affiliation. Males and
young people with no religious ties hold more liberal views
on necking, petting, and sexual relations. Young Canadian
females — attitudinally, at least — tend to associate sexual
involvement with meaningful relationships. Some 60% do
not approve of sexual relations in dating settings (vs. 30%
of males), while 25% do not approve of premarital sex,
even when the people involved love each other (vs. 17% of
males). In Herold's words: "For most women, being in a
love relationship is a prerequisite to engaging in premarital intercourse. Women have been conditioned to associate love with sex and are less willing than men to engage
in sexual relations solely for obtaining physical pleasure."[9]

During his 1984 visit to Canada, Pope John Paul re-
affirmed the Roman Catholic Church's teaching on premarital sex. "Naive sexual liberalization," he said, is "just
as dangerous and deadly as hallucinatory drugs."[10] Despite
the Pope's teaching, which is shared by many Protestant
churches, more than half of the teenagers who identify
themselves as Protestants or Catholics approve of sexual
relations after "a few dates". Those teenagers who not
only identify themselves as Catholics or Protestants but
who also participate in church life regularly are more conservative. Thirty percent of Catholics who attend and

approximately 21% of Protestants who actively attend church approve of intercourse after "a few dates". The most liberal views on premarital sex are held by young people with no religious affiliation (see Table 5.1).

The premarital sex mood, then, appears to be one of indulgence, with or without love. The rock group Kiss, in their hit song "Lick It Up", capture that mood with lines like "Don't wanna wait til you know me better."[11]

The arena of teenage sexuality, however, is not without its problems. Among its consequences have been venereal disease, unwanted pregnancies, and abortions. While adolescents have seemingly been more sexually active than their parents were as teens, a majority still are not regularly and responsibly using effective means of birth control. Some 50% may be engaging in premarital sex, but only half of that group are making use of contraception.[12] It seems apparent that many adolescents are sexually active but sexually illiterate. In the words of one Quebec survey respondent:

> People think teenagers are well informed about sex, but this is not the case.

Birth-Control Information

Canadian young people are nearly unanimous (93%) in maintaining that birth-control information should be available to teens who want it (see Table 5.2). Opposition to birth-control information constitutes a minority within virtually every sector of Canadian society. For example, only 7% of Catholic teenagers are opposed to the availability of such information.

The only debate seems to centre on who should do the educating and to what extent information should be linked to the availability of birth-control devices. School authorities' adding of sex education to the curriculum immediately prompted differences of opinion between parents and teachers and sometimes between educators themselves.

University of Guelph family studies professor Sam Luker has observed that the root of the controversy has not been sex education. Rather, "the root is that we are very nervous about sex in this country."[13] Some parents viewed the move as an invasion into family rights and responsibilities. They contended that it is impossible to educate about sex without also communicating moral and belief biases. Principals and teachers countered with the claim that many parents were silent on the subject and had abdicated giving information and counsel about this crucial area of life.

A recent national Gallup Poll has documented such an argument.[14] Only about 20% of Canadian adults say that their parents had discussed "the facts of life" with them before they reached the age of twelve. More than 60% say that they would have liked to have had more information about sex when they were growing up. Research by Edward Herold and Marilyn Goodwin has led to the conclusion that parents tend to provide neither birth-control information nor legitimation, leaving those roles to the adolescent peer group,[15] a point that is illustrated by a sixteen-year-old from Vancouver:

> As a child who found out "how to have a baby" when I was twelve years old, and not by my parents or any family members, but by a friend, I think that schools should teach us more about sex.

Even more poignant is the revelation of an Alberta sixteen-year-old:

> I wish information about birth control would be more readily available. If it was I probably wouldn't have had to have an abortion.

From a grade eleven Newfoundland female comes this observation:

> I think information on birth control should be available to all young people. It should be provided in school. Especially in high school. I think many of the unwanted

pregnancies would not have happened if there was information on birth control available to them.

It appears that public opinion now supports the position that sex education be available in schools. The aforementioned Gallup Poll on sex education revealed that 83% of Canadians are in favour of teaching sex in the classroom. Presently, close to half of the country's school districts offer "family life education" programs, with many of the rest planning to implement them. Such programs are more common in urban (more than 80%) than rural (about 25%) schools.[16]

Beyond birth-control *information,* it is apparent that birth-control *devices* are also increasingly available. During a special "Birth Control Week" in 1984, Toronto health department authorities offered to give away 10,000 sex kits—which included condoms—to teenagers. Their rationale was to draw attention to the increasing levels of pregnancy among girls fifteen to nineteen. In 1975 the rate for that sector was 7.5%. By 1982 it had risen to 9.6%. Organizers expressed alarm that some 70% of those pregnancies ended in abortions. The appeal was made to "play it safe".

If raising awareness about teenagers being sexually active was an objective of the program, then it was successful. The media gave the ensuing controversy national exposure. If giving away condoms was the reason for the plan, then it failed. There apparently was little necessity. Only 100 kits were picked up.

Abortion

Few social issues have generated as much controversy in recent years as abortion. The Supreme Court of Ontario acquittal in 1984 of Dr. Henry Morgentaler on abortion-related charges has only served to intensify the debate, with a myriad of interest groups involved in the fray. In

TABLE 5.2   Sexual Attitudes by Gender and Religious Affiliation

"Please indicate whether you AGREE OR DISAGREE with these items dealing with moral issues"

(% Agreeing)

	Nationally		Males	Females	Prot.	R.C.	None
	Teens	Adults*					
Sex before marriage is all right when people love each other	80	74	84	77	75	81	94
Birth control information should be available to teenagers who want it	93	95	92	95	93	93	98
It should be possible to obtain a legal abortion when a female has been raped	86	86	87	86	86	83	96
It should be possible for a married woman to obtain a legal abortion when she does not want to have any more children	39	47	41	36	41	28	65
Sexual relations between two people of the same sex is sometimes all right	26	31	21	31	22	26	43
Homosexuals are entitled to the same rights as other Canadians	67	70	54	80	66	68	77
It is sometimes all right for a married person to have sexual relations with someone other than their marriage partner	12	21	17	8	10	10	24

*Adult data drawn from Bibby, 1982.

late November of 1984, Emmett Cardinal Carter, the Roman Catholic archbishop of Toronto, urged his congregation of more than 1.1-million to fight laws that "do not sufficiently protect the unborn". He stated, "Even where partial protection is afforded, the law is being flouted."[17]

However, despite the controversy over abortion, Canadian teenagers are nearly unanimous in maintaining that legal abortion should be a possibility under some circumstances. Specifically, close to 9 in 10 young people say that it should be possible for a woman who has been raped to obtain a legal abortion (see Table 5.2). There is no difference in attitudes between males and females. And, significantly, there is little difference between young Catholics and others.

Some teenagers favour leaving the issue up to the pregnant woman, regardless of factors behind the pregnancy. A sixteen-year-old female living in rural Manitoba comments:

> I am very much against the present Canadian abortion laws. The government should not be able to control a woman's body. What happened to "freedom of choice"??

A central Alberta male in grade eleven narrows his generalization to teenagers:

> All girls should be entitled to abortions. If they get pregnant, it can *destroy* the fathers' and mothers' lives.

However, many resist the idea of "abortion on demand". A sixteen-year-old Okanagan male argues:

> A fetus is a human and should have the same rights.

A grade ten female from Edmonton adds:

> Abortion is wrong. When going in for an abortion, you are killing a baby, not a piece of tissue.

Accordingly, teenagers are quite divided when asked if a legal abortion should be available to a married woman who does not wish to have more children. Here 39% say "yes" and 61% "no", with Roman Catholics (72%) more inclined than others to be opposed.

Homosexuality

The survey has found that, as a group, homosexuals are the number one target of teenage humour. The derision directed at homosexuals is evident in the common use of derogatory terms such as "fag", "faggot", and "lessie" in many parts of the country.

Seventy-four percent of Canadian teenagers feel that sexual relations between people of the same gender are wrong (see Table 5.2). However, this is not to say that young people favour discrimination against homosexuals. On the contrary, 7 in 10 maintain that homosexuals are entitled to the same rights as other Canadians. Males are somewhat more troubled by homosexuality than females (79% are opposed to such relations vs. 69%) and are also less reluctant to accord gay people basic human rights (54% in favour vs. 80% in favour for females). Teenagers with no religious ties exhibit less opposition to homosexuals.

Extramarital Sex

Teenagers show even less receptivity towards extramarital sex than towards homosexual relations. Some 88% feel such activities are not right. Indeed, 57% are *strongly* opposed to extramarital relations, compared with 48% for homosexuality and 7% for premarital sex involving love. Females are slightly more opposed to extramarital relations than are males (92% vs. 83%). The religiously unaffiliated once more are less opposed than those with religious ties (76% vs. 90%).

Young people are saying that they still believe in traditional monogamous marriage. Other data from the survey confirm that as they project their futures they hope and expect to get married. They are ready to embrace their heritage and build their lives around "love and marriage" and the family unit. They are not in favour of new forms that set the family aside.

Teenagers are making another statement in their opposition to extramarital sex. Adolescents have expectations of adults. According to the survey they are expecting their parents and other married adults to honour *their* commitments. Perhaps adolescents' convictions are the result of experiencing the consequences of infidelity in their own homes, or of seeing those consequences in the homes of their friends.

Teenagers vs. Parents: Revolution or Evolution?

For all the publicity and adult anxiety over the alleged unprecedented movement among today's young people towards sexual permissiveness and sexual radicalism, it is clear that Canadian teenagers differ little in attitude from their parents and other Canadian "grown-ups" (see Table 5.2). In the area of premarital sex, they do hold slightly more liberal views than older Canadians *presently do.* This is not to say, however, that even here a big change has taken place, for we do not know how Canadian adults felt about premarital sex *when they were teenagers* vs. *when they became parents of teenagers.* Otherwise, today's young people either have virtually identical attitudes (on birth-control information, abortion where pregnancy was caused by rape, homosexual rights) or are *more conservative* than adults (on homosexuality, extramarital sex, abortion when another child is not wanted — see Table 5.2). One grade ten student from Vancouver, a female, reflects the latter mood:

> I feel that the morals of today are very low. I find myself without respect for many of the people I am in contact with because of their moral beliefs. This includes my parents.

The alleged dramatic change in premarital sexual attitudes and behaviour is perhaps best understood as follows.

Researchers have found that by about 1965 changes were showing up in Gallup opinion polls and regional behavioural studies.[18] By the early 1970s, a major American national study revealed that since the sex research of Alfred Kinsey around the early 1940s, behaviour had changed significantly. More than 50% of men with some college education had experienced coitus by age seventeen, twice what Kinsey found. In the case of single women under twenty-five, 75% had had coitus, compared with only 33% in Kinsey's day. Among married women of ages eighteen to twenty-four, no less than 80% had had intercourse before marriage.[19]

These findings describe not today's teenagers, but their parents, who themselves went through their teens in the late 1950s and 1960s. What we appear to be seeing in the similarity of sexual views of Canadian teenagers and adults is neither an ongoing sexual revolution, nor a return to pre-revolutionary times, but, rather, the adults' transmission of *their own* sexual attitudes and practices to young people.

It seems apparent that today's teenagers are "little adults". They are conforming to the norms they perceive around them. Rather than being like sculptors who shape and create new forms, adolescents are more like sponges soaking up the prevailing standards in their environment.

In short, the evidence is light for the thesis that a sudden shift in sexuality took place with the post-World-War-II generation, only to be replaced by a move to the right with the present generation. The post-war shift is being perpetuated by the emerging generation. The pattern might better be seen as *sexual evolution* rather than a *sexual revolution*.

Censorship

There is also little reason to believe that Canadian teenagers differ significantly from adults when it comes to their views about pornography. The nation's adults have been fairly consistent since at least the 1970s in favouring

control, rather than outright banning, of the distribution
of pornographic materials. For example, a 1980–81 national
survey found that 57% favoured laws forbidding the distribution of pornographic materials to people under the age of
eighteen. Some 35% felt such materials should be banned,
and the remaining 8% favoured no restrictions at all.[20]

Young people basically seem to concur. They equally
favour no restrictions or censorship of nudity; only about
5% call for total banning (see Table 5.3). Explicit sexual
acts, they maintain, should be censored (56%) or not
restricted (31%); here only 13% feel total banning is appropriate. However, in the case of hard-core pornography,
where sex involves violence, more than 5 in 10 favour total
banning, while another 3 in 10 call for censorship controls.
Less than 20% feel that there should be no restrictions.

Teenagers who offer observations tend to be those at
the "total banning" or "no restriction" extremes. On the
"banning" side is a sixteen-year-old Newfoundland female
who says:

> I don't think you have to have filth in order to have
> fun.

An Alberta female in grade twelve is more specific:

> [Such materials] are partly responsible for the weirdos
> and perverts out in this world. Many get ideas from
> these and go rape girls, etc. It's sickening to know very
> vulnerable people are brainwashed.

On the "no censorship" side is another Atlantic province
student, a male, who comments:

> The decision should be up to the individual. Censor-
> ship and banning would just give the government more
> power.

In his camp is a grade twelve female from rural Ontario
who argues:

> By censoring we're only calling more attention to it. If

TABLE 5.3　Attitudes Towards Censorship of Sexual Materials by Gender and Religion (In %'s)

"Do you think there should be NO RESTRICTIONS, CENSORSHIP CONTROLS, or A TOTAL BANNING in the case of the following sexual materials?"

	NUDITY			SEXUAL ACTS			HARD CORE PORNOGRAPHY		
	Open	Censor	Ban	Open	Censor	Ban	Open	Censor	Ban
Nationally	47	47	6	31	56	13	16	30	54
Males	65	32	3	46	47	7	26	38	36
Females	31	61	8	15	65	20	8	21	71
Protestants	47	48	5	28	56	16	11	29	60
Roman Catholics	43	50	7	30	56	14	19	28	53
None	58	40	2	35	59	6	17	33	50

it's no big deal, people won't care and we'll have less hassle. Look at Europe and their nude beaches and monokinis.

While Protestants, Catholics, and the unaffiliated vary little in their attitudes on the dissemination of sexual materials, there are consistent, significant differences between males and females. Males take a far less restrictive position. They are more likely than females to favour no controls in the case of nudity (65% vs. 31%), no controls where sexual acts are involved (46% vs. 15%), and, again, to oppose banning in the case of hard-core pornography (64% vs. 29%).

The somewhat subtle gender differences that first became noticeable in our examination of the sources of happiness — where males continue to show more interest in *athletics* than females — and in the issues that trouble teens — where females show more concern with their *physical appearance* than males — and finally in attitudes concerning the appropriateness of *sexual involvement* — where males exhibited more openness to casual sex — take on an "uneasy explicitness" with these findings on sexual materials.

The feminists may well be correct in their contention that sexual materials typically focus on women as impersonal — indeed, inanimate — objects to be exploited and denigrated. Certainly our respondents seem to agree. A fifteen-year-old female from the Edmonton area notes:

> It's usually women who are discriminated against and made filthy.

Consequently, many concerned with the status of women in this country and elsewhere have declared war on pornography as a war against a blatant vestige of the unequal position of women in modern societies. To the extent that the coming generation of men continues to hold the views we have uncovered, it seems clear that equality of the sexes may well be a goal still distant in Canada.

But perhaps we should not be surprised. The aforementioned recent national survey of adults showed that 42% of women favoured the banning of pornographic materials compared with 29% of men. A major source of sexism among male teenagers in the sexual sphere thus seemingly lies with the sexism prevalent among male adults. We would do well to remember that teenagers do not publish *Playboy* and *Penthouse*. Neither do they produce and direct the X-rated movies and videos. The pornography business does not put profits into their pockets. Adults — usually *male* adults — are in charge. Adolescents are merely a target audience and, tragically, along with younger children, are sometimes the featured attractions.

The problems go beyond the much-publicized December 1984 issue of *Penthouse*, which gave ten pages to photographs of naked Japanese women, some bound by ropes and dangling apparently lifeless from trees. A federally commissioned study released in the summer of 1984 revealed that about 540 different sexually oriented magazines are sold in Canada, with an estimated retail value of $100-million a year. That does not include the flood of books, films, and sex aids.[21] In a commissioned federal poll conducted earlier the same year, 34% of adults aged eighteen to twenty-nine acknowledged that they had purchased what they regarded as a pornographic video cassette. Nevertheless, only 12% of Canadian adults polled said that they regard pornography as a problem in their communities, with 59% seeing it either as a small problem or no problem at all.

Assessment

The survey reveals that, as with values, Canadian teenagers tend to hold essentially the same sexual views as adults. Once more it is clear that our major institutions have very effectively transmitted the dominant sexual ideas to young people. One looks in vain for indications either of an ongoing sexual revolution or a conservative swing. Even with premarital sex, it seems safe to conclude that post-war changes in attitudes and practices have been passed on to the coming generation.

The media debates over the "sexual revolution" and "return to the right" may consequently largely involve academics and others speaking to each other. Furthermore, alleged rapid movements in one direction or the other may tell us more about the biographies of some of these "media stars" that they do about social reality. *Time* magazine writes that the "obsession with sex is over" and tells us that "many individuals are rediscovering the traditional values of fidelity, obligation and marriage."[22] One cannot help but wonder just exactly who it was who "was obsessed" and is now "rediscovering" conventional values. Academics? Journalists? Feminists?

Which women is *Toronto Star* columnist Lynda Hurst describing when she writes: ". . . it was women, surely, who enabled the great change in social mores to take place. It was they who eagerly embraced the politics of liberation . . . they who had swallowed whole the notion that sexual freedom . . . was liberating and therefore good." And is Germaine Greer really telling the majority of North American women anything new when she informs them that she has discovered that "no sex at all is better than bad sex"? As Joseph Katz, human development officer for State University of New York, points out, "There was a massive liberalization of attitudes going on in the seventies. Any turning back from that is surprising."[23]

One of the unfortunate results of adults playing up the "sexual revolution" rather than premarital sexual evolution, and now emphasizing the alleged "turn to the right", is that teenagers lose either way.

On the one hand, in emphasizing the sexual revolution, parents and other adults, themselves participants in the premarital evolution, hypocritically charge their teenagers with being a part of it. Meanwhile, assisted by a zealous media, they not uncommonly project a myriad of sexual possibilities on their offspring. After all, this is supposedly the era of "happy hedonism" — unrestrained sex in all its countless varieties. Teenagers are left holding the bill. One grade eleven Montreal female expresses "the cost" this way:

> I believe that because of all the nasty things that my parents hear about teenagers outside the house, I am more and more forbidden to do anything at all now. I would like to know why my parents are so strict, and also do they have this right to treat us strictly because of what they hear outside?

She is not alone. A Roman Catholic girl from Quebec City comments:

> I have never been able to go out with a guy and I am 17 years old, because my parents don't want me to.

From a small community in British Columbia comes this observation from another grade eleven female:

> Our minds aren't warped, or whatever. All teenagers shouldn't be grouped together — not all of us go out and get drunk every weekend or get abortions. It's just the adults who think that.

Yet, on the other hand, in now claiming that there has been a "turn to the right", adults write for themselves the age-old "we've been there and now know better" script — thereby discouraging teenagers from holding the attitudes and doing the things that they themselves did.

Penitent opinion leaders are, of course, joined by the Roman Catholic Church and a variety of other religious groups in advocating premarital sexual chastity. They have further allies in organizations such as Teen-Aid, a U.S.-based organization that "advocates telling teens that falling in and out of love is a lot less complicated if they haven't gone to bed together".[24]

The new-found biological ability of teenagers to procreate is fuelled by a society that sanctions sex as a recreational option. Our visual world has pushed the creed of "the more bare the better". Soap operas, TV, movies, and home videos have been intent on breaking the barriers of nudity, rape, and incest. Many of the most popular television shows seem to gain their status from the frequency of the sexual innuendoes in the script. Enticing, erotic ads send the message to "get active" sexually. As adults, we have offered adolescents a sex-oriented society that drives for immediate gratification. At the same time, many adults still call out for celibacy as the standard for young people. When what is happening inside teenagers is wrapped with the erotica of the daily experiences in our culture, the combination is potent.

The irony is that today's adolescents don't give evidence of being any different in their outlook and their behaviour from adults around them. For better or worse, Canada's young people give strong evidence of being very similar to their grown-up role models. Yet the alienation produced by the hypocrisy produces a familiar pattern: sexual matters can be shared with friends but have to be hidden from adults. Herold's Canadian research, for example, has found that some 75% of teenagers feel that their parents would be upset if they found out that their offspring were having intercourse. Only about 25% think their adolescent friends would give them such a response.[25] In the realm of their sexuality, teenagers are like mirrors on the wall of their society. Eleventh-hour rhetoric about revolutions and new insight is not likely to significantly alter their sexual styles.

6

FAMILY AND FRIENDS

Relationships That Matter Most

Mothers, fathers and kids aren't as close as they should be. This situation takes away from the fun that kids have with their friends.
— a grade twelve female from Kitchener

Turbulence on the Home Front

Relating to teenagers at home can be like watching television with the volume turned off. The images are there transmitting some impressions about what is going on, but one is left guessing about the specifics in the script. The following scene has been repeated millions of times in Canadian homes. The parents are at home, waiting and wondering.

11:30 P.M.
Dad: "When is Steve supposed to be home?"
Mom: "His regular Friday night curfew time — 12:30, I guess."

12:30 P.M.
Dad: "Well, I'm going to bed."

Mom: "I think I'll keep reading my book until Steve gets
        in. I'll join you soon."

1:20 P.M.

Mom: "Steve, is that you? Glad you're home. You're late.
        Where have you been?"
Steve: "Out with my friends."
Mom: "Which ones?"
Steve: "The regular group — you know."
Mom: "Where did you go?"
Steve: "We just drove around."
Mom: "What did you do?"
Steve: "Oh, nothin' much."
Mom: "For six hours? You just drove around for six
        hours?"
Steve: "Yep, that's about it. Good night. Don't wake me
        up. Tomorrow's Saturday. I want to sleep in."

In those moments parents would like to turn on the sound
and turn up the volume. They would dearly like to know
what is going on inside. As questions remain unanswered
parents tend to link silence with distance. As they keep
reaching out, they have a deep feeling their sons and daughters are pulling away.

From the outset of our analysis of the survey results, we
have seen that relationships are immensely valued by Canadian young people. Indeed, only freedom may be valued as
highly. Yet, as the above scene would underscore, the major
source of the friendship and love for teenagers is, for many,
not parents. Predictably, the adult feelings on the subject
are often mutual. A recent national survey revealed that
42% of Canadian adults with teenagers were finding their
offspring to be a cause for concern. Similar anxiety was
expressed by 29% of the parents of young children and by
21% of those whose sons and daughters were now adults.
While 94% of parents with only young children said they
were getting "a great deal" of satisfaction from them, the
satisfaction level dropped to 75% among parents whose
children included teenagers.[1]

Teenage turmoil makes many parents wish that they could go back to changing diapers. The trauma that emergence produces for teenagers spills over into their parents' lives. Compared with the present, the past seems serene. Stubbornness, rudeness, conflict, and defiance come out of the mouths of previously pleasant babes and children. Ordinary conversation can be a strain. One's best intentions in the form of simple comments, the giving of time, the buying of clothes, and the giving of money can all be "gobbled up", not only with ingratitude but also with hostile displeasure. The words are ignored. The ride is expected. The clothes are not right. The money is inadequate.

There is more. At most it is difficult and at minimum it is annoying for adults to have to cope with the constant assault on their self-image. No one enjoys being treated as a bumbling incompetent who is out of touch with the world. When the implicit suggestion or explicit accusation comes from a budding human being, it is especially upsetting.

It would not be so bad if parents could emotionally detach themselves from their offspring, but such a "blacking out" is seldom possible. As the authors of *Toughlove* point out, "We are hooked into our children and we cry and laugh, mourn and rejoice with them. They can tug at our heartstrings, delight us, or make us anxious and distraught in an instant. Their power to influence us, particularly as adolescents in crisis, is no less than our power to influence them ... No one can upset parents like their children."[2]

Often the prevailing feeling among parents is one of helplessness, the prevailing sentiment one of frustration, the prevailing thought, "What is happening?" Parents throw up their hands remembering better days when kids were younger and life was simpler.

As we have been emphasizing, experiencing emergence in a world controlled by adults is very difficult for teenagers. Adults are frequently insensitive to the reality of emergence. Young people are gradually becoming less dependent on adults. Accordingly, they want to be free to make an ever-increasing number of decisions themselves. Parental directives are therefore commonly received as attacks on teenage autonomy. Parents' authority is challenged. Tempers erupt. Parents talk but they do not listen. They give time and do favours when it suits their schedules. They buy clothes without consulting their daughter or son (teenagers, just once, would like to be able to do the reverse, and see what happens). Parents have money for the things they want: eating out, films, concerts, and even tapes and videos. Yet they think they are building character by giving adolescents not quite enough or barely enough money.

The result is that teenage emergence is often far from an enjoyable experience for both young people and adults. The experience falls far short of the co-operative, mutually sensitive ideal we are advocating.

But teenagers and adults alike *do* want rewarding relationships. Both want companionship and love. Consequently, they frequently turn elsewhere. Adults look to other adults and younger children. Teenagers turn to other teenagers who are "in their world" and comprehend what they are going through. A sixteen-year-old female from rural Quebec sums it up:

> We are hard to understand, yet we do understand each other.

The Supplementary Role of Friends

Nothing is of greater importance to adolescents than friendship. It is highly valued by 9 in 10 Canadian young people. Further, 3 in 4 report that they receive high levels of personal gratification from their friends. In fact, as we saw in Chapter Three, friends are the most commonly cited source of enjoyment.

During adolescence the peer group is a major source of

self-esteem. It provides young people with emotional security, support, information, and feedback as they build their own identities.[3] Take information, for example. Adults are ignorant of many aspects of life that matter to teenagers, like the latest fads. Moreover, sensitive topics such as sex, looks, and loves are easiser to discuss with peers. The fact that some of the information provided might be the wildest misinformation in no way minimizes its importance to the young people involved.[4]

Teenagers, it is well known, typically have "friendship clusters". The survey shows that about half of Canada's teens have four or more close friends. Most of the remaining half report that they have two or three. Less than 5% have no one they would call a close friend. Research suggests that this "friendless minority" commonly have problems, lacking self-confidence and being treated with indifference and cruelty by other adolescents. Isolated teenagers are more likely to have mental problems, be delinquent, and be under-achievers in school.[5]

To be sure, teenage friendship ties are often as precarious as romantic ties. Studies of the stability of friendships indicate an increase in friendship fluctuations at about thirteen and fourteen, followed by a decline in fluctuations to age eighteen. After eighteen, friendship fluctuations again increase, due primarily to geographical movement, jobs, or marriage.[6]

As we have been stressing, the value teenagers place on friendships with other teenagers would not be so disconcerting if they similarly valued their relationships with their families. But, for many, such is not the case. Peers matter more — a lot more. As previously noted, 91% place friendship on the top rung of their value ladders, whereas only 65% say that family life is "very important" to them. On the enjoyment scale, friends win again. Almost 75% claim to receive high levels of enjoyment from their friends, in contrast to less than 45% for their fathers and mothers.

Of course this is not to say that the family is not highly

valued or enjoyed, or viewed as a major influence in young people's lives. But it is to say that during these early years, teenagers depend greatly on their friends for the happiness and love that they readily acknowledge to value.

Rather than following the predominant folk wisdom and giving parents an exemption from responsibility in the existing alienation, our emergence thesis suggests a second possibility. Given that teens continue to value relationships and love, they may commonly turn to their friends because they have little choice. They are unable to experience with their parents the relationships and emotions that they value. Our findings consistently point to the major area of contention: *freedom*.

Teens evolving into full-grown human beings require considerable growing room in the form of comprehension, receptivity, and compassion. A major source of conflict and alienation would seem to rest with the central issue of whether or not parents and other adults have the capacity and the willingness to let such emergence take place. Clearly, this is often not the case. Young people are forced to gravitate towards friends, not as a means of *complementing* the good things they experience with parents but as a *subcultural substitute* for the understanding, acceptance, and direction not received at home. They frequently have a similar experience of lack of understanding with other adults, and feel equally alienated from institutions such as the school and church. As educator Baughman puts it, "Denied so many adult world opportunities and advantages, the young person sees the peer group as a substitute for adult status, productivity, and achievement. With his own age mates of similar interests and background, he finds opportunities to establish status and demonstrate what he can do."[7] Sociologist Hans Sebald similarly writes that "the youth culture is a social reaction to the young individual's uncertain status in the adult world."[8]

We do not mean to imply that teenagers form a rigid, separate world where they are cut off from adults and are in opposition to them.[9] The survey has already documented that this is not the case, that teenagers concur with dominant adult values and know appreciable social and emotional ties. Yet we disagree with the recent observation of the University of Waterloo's Frank Fasick that adolescent affection levels towards parents remain largely unchanged, and that peer relationships represent primarily an extension rather than a supplanting of "warm ties of affection" with parents. Instead we agree with and would underline one of Fasick's own observations (which he proceeds to minimize): "Some attenuation in bonds with parents, however, may occur in late adolescence."[10]

Friend and Family Influence

Sociologist Marlene Mackie of the University of Calgary points out that "the family's impact upon the child transcends all the other agents of socialization," and that peers "constitute the second most potent socialization agency".[11]

TABLE 6.1 *Perceived Sources of Influence (In %'s)*

"To what extent do you think your life is influenced by:"

	A Great Deal	Quite a Bit	Some	Little or None	Totals
The way you were brought up	55	30	11	4	100
Your own will power	43	39	15	3	100
Your friends	30	43	23	4	100
Chars. you were born with	24	36	29	11	100
God or some supernatural force	16	20	31	33	100
What people in power decide	12	27	38	23	100
Your teachers	9	32	43	16	100
The media	8	26	45	21	100
Luck	5	16	45	34	100

Young people are well aware of this influence of family and friends. More than 50% acknowledge that their lives have been influenced by "the way they were brought up", while about 30% say the same about the current impact of their friends (see Table 6.1). Only about 10% view their teachers, or "people in power", or the media as having a high level of influence on their lives. In fact, approximately the same importance is given to "God or some other supernatural force". Few give much credence to luck.

Along with one's upbringing and friends, the two other factors perceived as critical are one's own will power and biologically-acquired characteristics. *Family, friends,* and *self,* then, are viewed as the key determinants of a teenage life.

However, while the family is seen as having had a profound influence in shaping who young people are, its perceived impact at this point in their lives, as we have seen, appears to be secondary to friends.

Such an assertion is consistent with the conclusions of a recent synthesis of studies dealing with the sources of influence among North American youth.[12] The analysis revealed that in 1960 teenagers were influenced primarily by parents. Friends were ranked number three. By 1980 parents were number two, with friends moving up to the number one position. Grandparents and extended family members, who ranked seventh in 1960, had dropped to number ten by 1980. In other categories, teachers fell from two to four, the clergy from four to six, and youth group leaders from five to nine.

These findings suggest that the individuals and institutions most "in tune" with teenage emergence are those that potentially have the greatest impact on them. Clearly the family still has a critical primary group influence. But friends, seemingly more in touch with the experience of teenagers, have even more.

It is important to remember that parents and peers differ in the areas of a teenage life they influence. The input of parents is more likely to be taken seriously in areas such as values and beliefs, rather than in areas such as fashion, language, and social activities, where peer influence is strong. At the same time, because peer group members commonly have similar family backgrounds, peer influence undoubtedly reinforces parental influence.[13] As Fasick puts it, precisely because the peer culture "is constructed primarily of nonessentials, participation in it does not imply rejection of adult-related values . . . "[14]

In probing the sources of influence, we do not mean to imply that teenagers are mere puppets being manipulated by friends, parents, and others. Quite the opposite. We have just seen that teenagers maintain that they themselves have a primary place in influencing what happens in their lives. Only a minority say that the statement, "I usually do what my friends want me to do," describes them very well (4%) or fairly well (29%). In fact, 2 in 3 claim that "I sometimes feel that I am different from my friends." A grade eleven female from Saint John, New Brunswick, comments:

> If my friends want me to go somewhere with them I will. But if they wanted to do something I felt was wrong, I wouldn't participate. I'd also give them my opinion. I am the kind of person who can make up her mind and make her own decisions.

A sixteen-year-old from the Edmonton area says:

> My friends often influence my actions, but if there is something I feel isn't right or shouldn't be done, *I don't do it.*

A grade twelve student from Regina offers this insightful view of choosing friends with similar outlooks rather than merely being shaped by their outlooks:

> Usually what I want to do and what my friends want to do are one and the same thing. That's why they are my friends. They never force me or encourage me to do

things I don't feel are right, or to do things that will harm my physical being (drugs or drinking when I don't want to).

Further, a grade eleven female from Ontario takes the position that teens are responsible for peer friend selections:

I don't take peer pressure as an excuse for doing anything. If a person is strong enough and mature enough to make her own decisions, she should be able to decide not to hang around people that force her into something.

When assessing the influence of friends, it is also important to keep in mind that teenagers, like adults, are not an homogenous, monolithic group. To speak of "peer influence" is to speak of a variety of peer-group possibilities. Generally speaking, researchers find that at least three subcultures exist in an average North American high school.[15] First, there is *the fun subculture*, focusing on extracurricular activities. Second, there is *the academic subculture*, characterized by an emphasis on getting good grades. (While the "bookworm" is still scorned, the bright student who gets A's without studying is admired and envied, especially if also involved in extracurricular activities.)[16] Third, there is *the delinquent subculture*, comprised of those who rebel against the school, academically and socially.

Clearly, however, these are just main categories or "ideal types". Many other variations can readily be found. For example, research into the trend-setting groups in one suburban high school in the northeast of the United States revealed that three dominant groups of this kind were present. The "jocks" were athletically minded, drank a lot, and almost never smoked dope. The "motorheads" were primarily males noted most for their cars, leather jackets, low grades, and different hair-styles. The "flea bags" used drugs regularly, usually marijuana, and spoke of getting "wasted" and "baked". Many other students did not fit into any of these three groups.[17]

It is apparent from their complaints about adult stereotyping that Canadian teenagers frequently find themselves being labelled and mistrusted because of the publicized deviance of some young people. As with behaviour, the types of friendship groupings actually vary dramatically.

The Impact of Different Family Structures

Divorce rates have soared in Canada since 1960. At that time the rate was 1.7 per 1,000 married women; by 1980 the rate stood at 10.5. (This annual rate of 10.5 per 1,000 married women may seem low compared with the oft-cited statistic that 1 in 4 marriages end in divorce. This latter statistic, however, refers to the culmination of the former rate over a period of years.) The increase can be directly attributed to a liberalization of the Divorce Act in 1968. Indirectly, the jump reflects a society in which divorce has become more socially acceptable and more feasible as an alternative to an unhappy marriage.[18]

Yet, family sociologist Emily Nett of the University of Manitoba reports the somewhat surprising census finding that the percentage of one-parent families has actually changed very little in the 70 years such census statistics have been gathered. This is primarily because of remarriage. Given that the average marriage ending in divorce lasts only ten years, many Canadians remarry in their thirties. By 1979, 14% of annual brides had been previously married.[19] A central question raised by lay person and academic alike is, What are the consequences of such a marriage, divorce, and remarriage pattern for the children involved?

Reflecting the characteristics of the Canadian population, 82% of the teenagers in our sample come from homes where their parents (including step-parents) are married. Another 8% report that their parents are divorced, and 4% indicate that they are separated. The remainder are from homes where one parent (5%) or both parents (under 1%) are not alive, or where their parents are not married (1%).

The folk wisdom is that changes in the traditional family structure are having severe negative consequences both for young people and our society. Children of divorced parents are typically viewed with scepticism by people within our major institutions. Teachers have been known to discriminate against them, while clergy and church members have been wary both of them and their parents. In David Elkind's words, "Teachers and administrators . . . frequently expect that a child from a divorced family is going to have problems. Likewise, any difficulty the child does encounter is immediately attributed to the family problem without any consideration of possible other problems, such as, say, poor vision."[20] The national survey findings allow us to explore some of the correlates of different family structures.

Family and Friends

Young people whose parents are divorced differ little from others in the value they place on love, friendship, and family life (see Table 6.2). Some 1 in 4 teenagers whose parents are *divorced or separated* indicate that they worry a great deal about their parents' situation. About 1 in 10 teenagers whose parents are *together* indicate that they also worry a great deal about their parents' marriage. In the words of one family expert, "When there is upset in the family of the adolescent, whether the parents divorce or remain unhappily married, the effect is disturbing." He suggests that this "is one reason why so many youths seek love and companionship . . . with others outside their own family".[21]

Significantly, however, despite the differing levels of concern about their parents' marital problems, adolescents from one-parent situations do not indicate that loneliness is a greater problem for them than it is for others. In fact,

TABLE 6.2 *Attitudes and Reported Enjoyment, Family and Friends, by Marital Status of Teenagers' Parents (In %'s)*

	Married	Divorced	Separ.	Widowed	Nationally
Viewed as "Very Important"					
Being loved	88	83	85	87	87
Friendship	91	94	84	91	91
Family life	67	58	62	64	65
Bothered "A Great Deal" by					
My parents' marriage	9	23	27	—	11
Loneliness	15	17	18	15	15
Enjoy "A Great Deal"					
Friendships	74	72	78	74	74
Mother	46	46	51	46	46
Father	42	32	29	22	39
Sister	26	23	23	30	26
Brother	26	29	23	29	26
Grandparents	27	30	33	27	28
The Future					
Will marry	86	85	73	84	85
Will have children	88	86	79	89	85
Family will lose influence	56	56	61	60	56

perhaps surprisingly, they report that they receive appreciable levels of enjoyment from *both* their father and their mother, even though one is not physically present. Research suggests that the difference in gratification that does persist is the result, over the long haul, of offspring becoming closer emotionally to the parent with whom they are living, usually the mother (she is the custodial parent of more than 85% of children involved in divorce).[22] One cost of divorce for many fathers and some mothers is the loss of closeness, regardless of the reasons behind the divorce.[23]

While teenagers from homes involving divorce do report slightly higher levels of gratification from mothers than fathers, they do not show a tendency to compensate for the physical loss of one parent through greater involvement than other adolescents with brothers and sisters or grandparents.

Teenagers who have lost a parent through death also differ little from others in valuing family and friends and in experiencing considerable enjoyment from both. Further, family structure has little bearing on the future marriage and child-bearing plans of these teenagers, along with the way in which they view the future of the family.

The major exception to this uniformity in attitude and experience is the grouping of teenagers who come from homes where their parents are *separated* (see Table 6.2). Such a transitional status does not mean that there is any less tendency to value family life and being loved. However, precisely because it is valued, the offspring of separated parents show a slightly greater tendency to turn to friends and to the parent they are living with (usually the mother), along with grandparents, and to be alienated from the parent who is gone (usually the father). In addition, they are slightly less hesitant to indicate that they themselves plan eventually to marry and have children. They also are somewhat more sceptical about the future of the family generally.

These findings suggest that teenagers from established settings — that is, where a family arrangement is fairly permanently fixed, with two adults or one adult present — differ little from each other in their outlook on the family and in the gratification they report receiving from family members. Offspring from settings involving divorce and death show no inclination either to overcompensate with other kinds of social ties or to be undercompensated by them. The situation that is most disruptive for relationships is the separated, "non-established" setting.

Values

Family structure appears to make little difference to the inculcation of typical "middle-class" values. Teenagers from environments where divorce, separation, and death are involved differ negligibly from other Canadian young people in the importance they give to themes such as honesty, hard work, politeness, and cleanliness (see Table 6.3).

Self-Image

Further, teenagers without two married parents do not give evidence of feeling that they are either less socially competent or less physically and socially attractive than other youth. The survey does provide, nevertheless, an

TABLE 6.3 *Values, Self-Image, and Outlook by Marital Status of Teenagers' Parents (In %'s)*

	Married	Divorced	Separ.	Widowed	Nationally
Values:					
"Very Important"					
Honesty	86	84	82	82	85
Working hard	69	70	68	61	69
Politeness	65	67	63	57	65
Cleanliness	78	80	77	82	79
Self-Image:					
Highly Positive					
Social competence*	26	31	25	21	26
Looks and popularity**	36	36	38	33	35
Feel inferior	28	29	34	33	29
Outlook					
Happiness: High	27	18	15	19	26
Low	9	16	22	18	11

*"I find it easy to speak out in class."
**"I'm as 'nice looking as other people' and 'well-liked as most people'."

interesting finding: despite the fact that teenagers whose parents are not living together report both (1) similar gratification from relationships and (2) similar views of competence as teenagers from two-parent homes, *as a whole* they are slightly *less likely* to see themselves as happy compared with other Canadian teenagers (see Table 6.3). Apparently "the national family structural norm" continues, at least in some cases, to take its social–psychological toll. Even when offspring seemingly vary little on gratification from relationships and their physical and social attributes, their different family structural status is sometimes not without some negative effects. As sociologist Nett points out, "The stigma may be more harmful to children than the condition" of living with only one parent.[24]

Lifestyle

It is widely recognized that conventional marriage has a number of conventional correlates when it comes to how life is viewed and lived. For example, research shows a high correlation between marriage and various types of involvement in other associations with both in turn highly related to traditional views of morality.

Our survey shows that in areas such as *school work* and *recreation*, young people vary little by the marital status of their parents (see Table 6.4). The variations that do exist are fairly predictable in the light of our earlier findings. Teenagers from separated settings show a slight tendency to have their school work affected by their parents' marital problems. Adolescents whose parents are divorced are slightly less likely to engage in the family-centred activity of TV watching than others.

However, when one turns to the *group involvement* and *morality-related issues*, differences by family structure are apparent. Teens from settings with only one parent present are less likely than others to play team sports and participate in youth groups. Those whose parents are divorced or separated are also less inclined to attend reli-

TABLE 6.4 *Select Lifestyle Characteristics by Marital Status of Teenagers' Parents (In %'s)*

	Married	Divorced	Separ.	Widowed	Nationally
Conventional Activities					
Read books	29	33	26	29	29
Spend time on a hobby	35	35	35	32	34
Sit and think	44	49	48	49	44
Attend parties	39	43	44	40	40
Workout	37	39	39	35	37
Go to a video games arcade	13	11	16	18	13
Watch television	58	49	58	51	57
Enjoy school	15	17	13	16	16
Do homework	48	43	34	52	47
Associations					
Play team sports	41	37	33	33	39
Participate in youth groups	18	13	15	11	17
Attend religious services	25	9	16	19	23
Student union involvement	10	11	2	11	10
Other club executive	20	19	10	15	19
Moral Issues					
Premarital sex: all right	79	91	86	85	80
Sex all right, by few dates	51	64	58	55	52
Homosexuals: civil rights	66	76	68	77	67
Abortion: children unwanted	37	53	45	45	39
Use drugs	16	24	30	18	17
Smoke cigarettes	17	31	28	21	19
Drink alcohol	23	26	26	27	23

gious services. In part this would seem to reflect the reduction in a family's social network when divorce and death occur. The social ties are fewer. It may also be indicative of the fact that many organizations, consciously and unconsciously, aim their programs at two-parent families. The pattern may further be a commentary on the stigma young people feel when participating in such nuclear family-oriented activities.

With respect to morality-related issues and activities, teenagers from homes with only one parent physically present — essentially "fatherless" homes — are somewhat more likely to hold more liberal sexual views and to admit to using drugs, including alcohol and tobacco (see Table 6.4). These findings are consistent with a recently published study of adolescents in a large U.S. city.[25] The authors of this study found that the absence of the father from the home resulted in greater use of alcohol and marijuana, as well as in higher levels of sexual activity, especially in the case of males. They maintain that their results point to the ongoing significance of the father as a key figure in the transmission of values and as a deterrent to certain behaviour. Interestingly, they found that fathers are seldom turned to when young people seek direction in the areas of either drugs or sex. Their role would seem to be typically one of authority figure rather than empathetic advisor.

Assessment

The family continues to have a significant impact on Canadian young people. However, influence is one thing, enjoyment another. The survey reveals that many teenagers tend to find high levels of gratification from friends rather than from their mothers and fathers. They consequently place more value on friendships than they do on family life.

We repeat our thesis: to the extent that adults are sensitive to the reality of teenage emergence and help to facilitate it, much of the conflict between the generations can be averted. More positively, the teenage years can be mutually enjoyable ones.

Our findings suggest that, as a whole, teenagers from homes of divorced, separated, and widowed parents differ very little from other teenagers. Considering the conflict and pain commonly associated with divorce and death, the ability of young people to adjust to their altered circumstances is often remarkable. Once removed from the limbo of separation, children of divorced parents, along with the widowed, hold attitudes about the future that are not dampened by their situations at home. Their feelings about getting married, having children, and family life generally remain undaunted. In the case of those from divorced situations, their feelings of gratification from the so-called "missing" parent are also held at a healthy level. It appears that in a society where two parents are the norm, offspring of the divorced cope well if they can feel secure with one parent and know that the other is not gone from their world.

Family expert F. Philip Rice sums up the complex relationship between family structure and its consequences for young people. He says the overall effect depends on the conditions of the divorce and on events before and after it. When there is little fighting between parents during and after the divorce, and when the children have free access to both parents and emotional support from parents, siblings, and friends, the upset is kept to a minimum. In situations where divorces are bitterly fought and children are used as pawns, scapegoats, allies, and spies, a wide range of emotional problems result. Rice concludes that "other things being equal, a happy unbroken home is better for adolescents than a happy broken home, and that both are better than an unhappy, unbroken home, or an unhappy, broken home."[26]

To the extent that teens from homes with one parent do feel less happy and confident than other young people, the culprit in large part seems to be society. Ironically, by treating such adolescents as if they are different, by stigmatizing them, society in some instances tragically "succeeds" in making them feel different from others their age.

7

BELIEFS:

The Place of Religion in Teenage Lives

I only go to church on special occasions but I do strongly believe in God!
— a seventeen-year-old female from Toronto

The Persistence of Religion

As recently as the 1960s, the secularization of North America seemed obvious. Plummeting church attendance, experienced first by Protestants and then by Roman Catholics, seemed predictable in a society in which the phrase "God is dead" sounded appropriate. The earlier predictions of Sigmund Freud and others — that modern men and women would abandon religion in favour of rationality, "leaving heaven to the angels and the sparrows" — were seemingly being realized. Religion was giving way to reason, and things would never be the same.

Now, only two decades later, it is apparent that rationality has not slain human intrigue with supranatural phenomena. Interest in "reality beyond the senses" is widespread. A careful analysis of the beliefs and practices of Canadian adults across this century has not revealed a tendency to abandon interest and involvement in things supranatural but simply a tendency to focus on *different kinds of supranatural phenomena*, in keeping with current cultural offerings.[1] For example, older Canadians express more decisive beliefs in traditional Christian ideas — God, the divinity of Jesus, life after death — than do younger Canadian adults. Yet the latter, rather than abandoning the supranatural, are more inclined than the former to give credence to astrology, psychic phenomena, and communication with the dead.

We have been emphasizing throughout this book that ideas are largely socially instilled. Our values and our attitudes are implanted through the socialization efforts of our major institutions. (Chapter Ten will discuss this process more thoroughly.) Beliefs are no different. We would expect that, as with values, the dominant beliefs of teenagers would be essentially the same as adults'. The key issue is what beliefs the major institutions and our pluralistic society are offering at any point in time. For as goes the menu, so go the choices.

At the same time, in keeping with our thesis, we would expect that any idea-instilling institution seen as suppressing emergence would tend to be resisted and, if possible, ignored.

Supranatural Beliefs

Despite the value placed upon science and sense-known reality, Canadian teenagers show little inclination to abandon supranatural notions. Close to 9 in 10 believe both in the existence of God and the divinity of Jesus (see Table 7.1). Approximately 4 in 10 further think that they have experienced God's presence. Nearly 8 in 10 say they believe in life after death, with only 5% ruling out such a possibility altogether.

Teenagers also give considerable credibility to psychic phenomena. Two in 3 maintain that "some people have special powers, enabling them to predict future events." In the words of one Ontario respondent:

> I really believe that humans have a sixth sense, or an extra dimension of perception, if that sounds plausible. The human mind is a far more complex piece of machinery and I don't think we've even begun to develop it to its fullest potential.

They also have a strong interest in astrology. Some one-third feel that "the stars, the planets, and the month we were born influence our lives." Communication with the dead is also seen as highly possible by 1 in 3 teenagers. Further, some 40% believe in the existence of "invisible forces" or "mysterious powers" that possess people or are found in places like houses.

Given that the media are a major source of ideas, we should not be surprised at these findings. Recent popular movies such as *Star Wars, Raiders of the Lost Ark, E.T.,* and *Return of the Jedi* were all brought to us in the "beyond" motif. Book stores have expanded their sections on the occult. Mystic comic book sales have soared. There is a growing fascination with transcendental experience. Esoteric forms of oriental meditation are offered as extension courses. Books on management theory are encouraging

TABLE 7.1 *Select Beliefs in Canada: Teenagers and Adults (In %'s)*

	Teenagers	Adults*
Existence of God	85	81
Divinity of Jesus	85	68
Life after death	80	69
Communication with the dead	36	38**
Some have psychic powers	69	58
Claims of astrology are true	37	45

*The adult data source for Tables 7.1–7.3: Project Can80.
**Data source: Project Canada.

executives to use their intuition in decision-making. ESP has new respect and status. There is talk about mental control over disease and ageing. Even universities are reflecting the intrigue with the supranatural. A number of prominent schools, including Stanford and Duke, have established institutes for psychical research. The interest of young people in such phenomena, therefore, is quite predictable.

As Table 7.1 shows, despite the negative prognostications of many an academic and lay person alike, the belief levels of Canadian teenagers, if anything, exceed those of adults. These findings are consistent with those for the U.S. where, despite a probable gradual increase in doubt, there is no indication that adolescence represents a time of widespread repudiation of traditional beliefs.[2]

Combined with the aforementioned findings concerning the persistence of supranatural beliefs among adults across this century, these data make the conclusion sound: the supranatural is not quite yet the prerogative of only "angels and sparrows".

Practices

Canadian young people not only are no less likely than Canadian adults to hold supranatural beliefs. They also show close to the same inclination to engage in various practices — with one critical exception.

Church Attendance. Approximately 1 in 3 adults with school-age children claim that their offspring are involved "regularly" in church activities.[3] Yet only about 1 in 4 Canadian teenagers say they "very often" attend religious services. This apparent discrepancy would seem to reflect the reality of the religious "drop-out" at this upper end of the "school-age" category. Five in 10 of the teenagers surveyed acknowledge that their present church involvement level is *less* than it was when they were younger. Two in 10 say it is now higher and 3 in 10 that it has not changed. Related to this, the percentage of those attending "very often" decreases from 25% for fifteen-year-olds to 23% for seventeen-year-olds to 15% for nineteen-year-olds. Significantly, weekly church attendance for Canadians eighteen to twenty-nine stands at 15-16%.[4]

On balance, then, despite the fact that as many as 1 in 3 have been fairly highly involved in churches, teenagers are seemingly becoming less involved as they get older. By the time they reach their early twenties, only about 1 in 6 are still very active.

As for the future, some of those who drop out by the end of their teens will become more active when they marry and have children, but others will not.[5] The former are like a grade ten Saskatoon female who says:

> Religion is important, but not too important for me right now. But it's like that for most teenagers. I suppose I will practise my faith more when I'm older because I'll probably understand it better.

The latter, who will probably not become active, include those who, because they have never been active, do not have a religion to return to. One grade eleven male from a small Alberta town is an example:

> I don't see where religion plays a part with us. I have never been to church in my life except for funerals and weddings. I am doing just as good or better than anyone else who has been going to church for years.

In either event, the current "pool" stands at only 25%, perhaps as much as 10% *below* the present proportion of adults attending services weekly.

Their View of Organized Religion. Teenagers exhibit "a polite posture" towards formal religion. A two-thirds majority indicate that they have a fairly high level of confidence in church leaders, similar to the confidence they accord educational, scientific, and judicial leaders. Such a level far exceeds the confidence shown government, labour, and media. Further, they infrequently make religion a target of humour.

At the same time, they are divided on the role religious leaders should play in Canadian society. Half maintain that clergy should "stick to religion" and not "concern themselves with economic and political problems". The other half disagree, feeling that religion should address itself to such everyday issues.

Religious TV Programs.   As is the case with Canadian adults,[6] young people show no tendency to substitute religious TV programs for religious service attendance. The survey has found that a meagre 2% of teenagers watch religious programs on television "very often". A further 6% say they "sometimes" do, but the overall majority either "never" (70%) or "seldom" (22%) catch such programs. Significantly, as in the case of adults, religious programming is watched primarily by the initiated: 67% of the small audience of teenage viewers are regular church attenders. Conversely, only 2% of teens who *never* attend church, often (.4%) or sometimes (1.6%) watch such programs; 91% say they "never" do. Religious programming thus appears to be primarily an activity that complements church involvement, not one that provides a substitute for it. It is worth noting briefly that religious music is enjoyed "a great deal" by only about 3% of teenagers, with 3 in 5 of these young people being regular church-goers. On the other hand, of those teens who frequently attend services, only about 10% say they highly enjoy religious music.

Devotional Practices.   Two in 10 teens say they frequently pray privately, with almost another 3 in 10 claiming to do so sometimes. The remaining half of the teenage population indicate that they either seldom (3 in 10) or never (2 in

TABLE 7.2 *Select Practices in Canada: Teenagers and Adults*

(% "Regular" or "Very Often")

	Teenagers	Adults
Service attendance	23	28
Watch religious programs	2	6
Pray privately	20	37
Read the Bible	5	8
Read my horoscope	25	33

10) pray. By comparison, twice as many adults — 4 in 10 — claim to pray frequently (see Table 7.2). Yet at the other extreme, virtually the same proportion of adults as teenagers (2 in 10) say they never pray.

Scripture reading is relatively rare among young people, but no more so than with adults. Only about 5% of teenagers say that they *often* read the Bible, as do 8% of adults. Almost 50% of teenagers acknowledge that they *never* read the Bible, just under the 55% figure for adults.

Interestingly, Canadian teenagers show no such reluctance to skim the newspaper to read their horoscopes. More than half say they read their horoscopes often or sometimes. Indeed, less than 20% "never" bother to scan their "readings".

Teenagers can undoubtedly cite their astrology sign more readily than a given book in the Bible and know more about the basics of sign characteristics than the basics of Judaic-Christian history. This is more than an impressionistic deduction. Asked if they know which of Jesus' disciples denied him three times, and given a choice of six names, only 41% could identify Peter. Another 33% admitted that they did not know, while the majority of the remaining 26% answered "Judas". Adults fare little better; only 52% of them could cite Peter.

Regional and Social Variations

An analysis of beliefs and practices by region, religious affiliation, and gender reveals only minor variations within the population. As with adults, teenagers in the Atlantic region are somewhat more likely and young people in B.C. less likely than others to hold *conventional beliefs* and to carry out related practices. Such differences, however, disappear when *non-conventional* ideas — belief in communication with the dead, psychic power, astrology — are involved. Protestants and Catholics differ little in their belief and practice patterns. Minor variations include church attendance (Catholics 28%, Protestants 26%) and regular Bible reading (Protestants 11%, Catholics 2%).

Predictably, those teenagers who claim no religious affiliation differ from others on conventional items, but *not* on unconventional ones. Females show a slight tendency to exceed male proportions *on every belief and practice measure, both conventional and otherwise.* This reflects the adult pattern[7] and opens the floodgates for a variety of environmental and biological explanations.

The Search for Meaning

Canadian young people give evidence of raising the so-called "ultimate questions" about life and death with more urgency than is characteristic of adults. Specifically, some 3 in 10 teens — compared with 2 in 10 adults[8] — say that they often think about how the world came into being, the purpose of life, the sources of happiness, the reason for suffering, what happens after death, and whether or not there is a God or Supreme Being. Further, 20% of teenagers say that they are bothered a great deal by the issue of life's purpose. Another 25% maintain that the question troubles them "quite a bit".

On the one hand, this higher level of interest in the meaning of existence is to be expected among younger people. Adults are more inclined to say that they no longer raise such questions, having earlier resolved them. On the other hand, the interest level supports our assertion that there is little evidence that Canadians young or old are abandoning their interest in supranatural phenomena, perhaps in part because they continue to raise "ultimate questions" that in many instances require non-naturalistic explanations.

The Importance Accorded Religion

We have already seen that acceptance by God is not among the most widely endorsed values. Some 40% of Canadian teenagers view it as very important — compared, for example, with about 90% who place a high value on friendship and 65% who similarly rate family life. Interestingly, almost 40% of teenagers also maintain that their lives are influenced in a noteworthy way by "God or some other supernatural force", considerably below the influence accorded friends (73%) or biological factors (60%).

However, despite this apparently low ranking given to religion, it would be a mistake to minimize the importance conventional religion appears to have in the lives of at least a minority of young people, including, possibly, many of the 40% just noted. We asked teenagers to describe the nature of their religion, using an item that had previously been administered to adults. The results are fascinating. The "religious self-images" that teenagers have are virtually proportionate carbon copies of the self-images of Canadian adults (see Table 7.3). Almost 40% view themselves as "committed Christians", while a small percentage are committed to other religions. An additional 25% are

TABLE 7.3 *Religious Self-Images in Canada: Teenagers and Adults (In %'s)*

"Which of the following comes closest to describing the nature of YOUR religion?"

	Teenagers	Adults
The Committed	39	43
"I regard myself as a committed Christian"	(37)	(41)
"I am deeply committed to a religion other than Christianity"	(2)	(2)
The A-Religious	22	25
"I have a mild interest in Christianity and other religions, but I do not see myself as deeply religious"		
The Inquisitive	4	7
"I find myself interested in a variety of religions, but not committed to any particuar one"		
The Innovators	10	4
Varied, write-in responses		
The Non-Religious	25	21
"I am not a religious person"		

"a-religious" or "inquisitive", interested in Christianity and other religions but not committed. Another 10% lean towards no particular religion. The remaining 25% see themselves as not religious.

In terms of religious self-image, then, the emerging generation differs negligibly from Canadian adults. There is good reason to believe that both their subjective religious self-images and their objective religious affiliations are largely being inherited, with minimal disruption or innovation. In addition to the findings on self-image, the survey has found that 87% of teenagers with Protestant parents claim to be Protestants. The same is true for 91% of teenagers from Roman Catholic homes. These are almost identical to the intergenerational retention figures for adults (91% in the case of Protestants, 86% in the case of Catholics).[9]

It should be emphasized that the extensiveness of this transmission of religious identity across generations in Canada means that it is extremely difficult for religious rivals to the established Protestant and Catholic groups to make significant inroads. Contrary to "the great cult scare" of the 1970s and 1980s, very few Canadians at any age level have been recruited by the so-called "new religions".[10] Only 2% of teenagers and just under 2% of adults presently have a strong interest in any such groups — with these commonly being TM, Zen, Moonies, and Yoga-related movements and hence often not viewed as actual religions.

Canada appears to be characterized by remarkable intergenerational stability in the areas of affiliation and commitment self-image.

Assessment

While almost every young person identifies with one religious group or another, we have seen that by the time they leave their teens, only about 1 in 6 are *regular* church attenders. The major reason may not be very mysterious. As we saw earlier, religious groups are *not* associated with high levels of enjoyment for teenagers. Less than 10% say that they receive "a great deal" of enjoyment from church or synagogue life. In fact, when we focus only on those who are regular service attenders, even here a mere 24% say they are receiving a high level of gratification from their ties with organized religion — far below what regular attenders report for music (69%), friendships (77%), and sports (45%).

This "lack of enjoyment" associated with organized religion, which leads in many cases to dropping out and in many other instances to passive participation is, in our minds, no accident. What it may commonly signal is the inability of religious organizations to cope adequately with teenage emergence. Here, as with the family and the school, teens "need room to become". If the room is given, there is no reason to predict that disenchantment and exodus is inevitable.

Historically the church has had a reputation for indoctrination rather than for encouraging enquiry and choice. Institutional religion is commonly seen, in sociologist Peter Berger's terms, as "sanctifying the status quo",[11] which for young people translates into sanctifying the adult world.

For example, Christian leaders have been accused of re-enacting the roles of the anxious mother or the authoritarian father in conveying morality and ethics.[12] Psychologist Edward Dreyfus points out that young people are "not supposed to seek their own truth because others have found it", that the church "expects students to accept the dictates of the administration on faith that everything will work out".[13] Some observers maintain that the tie between religion and parents is so strong that adolescents rebelling against parents may use religion as a means of striking out against them. For these young people, the rejection of religion is "a way of emancipating themselves from parents who are not giving them the freedom they seek".[14]

Related to this, parental imagery runs through Christianity: "Heavenly Father", "Holy Mother", "Child of God", "Brothers and Sisters". One result of such familial roles and imagery can be to make the church seem another part of life from which one needs to be freed in the course of becoming a full adult. As with real-life parents, the church has symbolized for many young people the repression of growth along a variety of the facets of emergence, notably the intellectual, social, sexual, and even spiritual dimensions. To the extent that teenagers come to use family imagery in the spiritual realm, rebellion against parents may also be associated with the collapse of religious faith.

Thus aligned with existing norms and institutions, organized religion has not gained the reputation of being a source of enjoyment and an ally in emergence for teenagers.

Understandably, then, organized religion is treated with a courtesy deemed appropriate for an older and irrelevant adult institution. However, it is increasingly abandoned as one crosses the bridge of adolescence and no longer is compelled to frequent church doors.[15] This general pattern of "polite detachment" yet ongoing identification with and consumer-like use of religious organizations mirrors dramatically the nature of adult religion in Canada.[16] It appears that such a style is being transmitted to the emerging generation with surprising thoroughness. Adults have shown little inclination to reject the religious affiliations of their parents. In keeping with their consumption habits in our highly specialized society, they have rather shown a tendency to draw very selectively from the increasingly diversified "religious menus" offered by their groupings. The available items range from traditional commitment through nominal attendance to the occasional rite of passage: a wedding, a baptism, a Bar Mitzvah, a funeral. They also draw on belief and practice "fragments" — belief in God, belief in Jesus, the occasional service, and the occasional prayer — rather than adopting entire religious "systems". Fragments, after all, are much more functional than all-embracing religions in a society encouraging compartmentalization and situationalism.

Consequently, few people switch affiliations or drop out, because increasingly it is not necessary or advantageous to do so. And as it is with Canadian adults, so it appears to be with Canadian teenagers. One eighteen-year-old Catholic comments:

> I wouldn't change my religion even if I don't approve
> of everything the Church does.

Teenagers readily adopt their parents' affiliation and religious self-image, along with some basic Judaic-Christian beliefs and selected practices. However, the majority neither profess religious commitment nor want extensive involvement with "their" religious groups. A grade ten female from rural Quebec says bluntly:

> I am Catholic, but I do not believe in what the priest says.

A sixteen-year-old female from a small New Brunswick town comments:

> I believe there is a God and an after-life but I don't believe you have to go to church to be a Christian.

To the extent that religious organizations are willing to accept such a situation, they assume a major service role. To the extent that the service role is rejected, groups find themselves in the somewhat peculiar situation of being the "identification group" of large numbers of Canadians who, through the power of intergenerational socialization, are extremely reluctant to turn elsewhere. Tennis star John McEnroe, in responding recently to the question "Are you religious?", articulated the position of this uncommitted, identification group: "I'm Catholic, but I'm not religious. I don't go to church any more. I used to until I was eighteen. Now I go once a year for my Mom at Christmas. I think Christmas is Mom's day so you do whatever she wants. If she wants me to go to church for an hour, it's not that bad."[17]

8

CANADA AND OTHER CANADIANS:

How Teenagers View Their Country

*The racial discrimination in Canada is disgust-
ingly high. Children learn what their parents
teach them. Thank God, I don't listen to my
father's prejudices.*

— a sixteen-year-old female from rural Newfoundland

So far, the focus of our analysis has been on the "micro"
level. We have concentrated on the emerging individual
teenager, particularly on his and her values, happiness
sources, personal concerns, sexuality, family and friends,
and beliefs. In this chapter, we want to move to the "macro"
level. We want to examine the Canadian teenager's relationship to the rest of the world, namely Canada and
beyond.

Intergroup Relations

Range of Social Ties

Canadian teenagers claim to have social contact with
people from a diversity of racial and ethnic backgrounds.

Their contacts with cultural minority members exceed that of adults in all instances, except for contacts with Jews. Some 6 in 10 young people outside Quebec say they are acquainted with at least one French-speaking Canadian, while teenagers in Quebec report the same proportion when asked about contact with English-speaking Canadians. Nationally, about 6 in 10 teenagers report that they are closely acquainted with one or more Black persons. Similar levels of contact are claimed by 5 in 10 in the case of Orientals, 4 in 10 regarding Canadian Indians, and 3 in 10 in the cases of East Indians–Pakistanis, and Jews.

Obviously the population distribution of minority groups results in varying opportunities for teenagers to mix with people of different backgrounds. As one grade twelve male, living in a small mining town in southern British Columbia, points out:

> I think that teenagers don't have the opportunity to meet new or different people (blacks, orientals, homosexuals, etc.) and thus develop their own beliefs and prejudices. I think this is mainly the situation for people who live in small communities.

Reflecting, in part, greater opportunities for interaction, contact with Blacks is somewhat higher in Ontario, while interaction with Orientals and East Indians–Pakistanis is greatest in B.C.

Yet accessibility alone, both nationally and regionally, clearly does not guarantee extensive contact. For example, only 34% of Ontario teenagers claim close association with East Indians and Pakistanis, while just 22% of young people in Quebec indicate such ties with Jews, despite the large East Indian–Pakistani and Jewish populations in Ontario and Quebec respectively. Such interaction patterns raise important questions about attitudes towards Canadian minorities.

Views of the Two Cornerstone Policies

Multiculturalism and bilingualism are the two pivotal policies guiding the federal government in its attempts to unite a Canada characterized by "the two nations", one anglophone the other francophone, and by ethnic diversity generally. In the main, the federal government's efforts to disseminate both policies as ideals appear to be highly successful.

Multiculturalism. Some 60% of teens say that they favour the "mosaic" model for Canada, in which, as the questionnaire explained, "people are loyal to Canada yet keep many of the customs of their previous countries" (see Table 8.1). In the words of one grade ten female from Edmonton:

> Canada is a land of many cultures and I feel everyone should be who and what they wish to be. Everyone should dress or practise traditions how they please or see fit.

Another 20% favour the "melting pot" model, in which people coming from other countries "give up their cultural differences and become Canadians". Most of the remaining 20% say that they have no preference either way. Only in Quebec do teenagers differ from the national norm. There, about 40% favour the mosaic and some 25% the melting pot. The main difference is that most of the rest (35%) say they have no preference.

Here again in Quebec, something of a "free spirit" towards the question of lifestyles that we have seen in our examination of values, sexuality, and beliefs is once more apparent. The Quebec teen attitude commonly seems to be, "Do what you yourself want." In the present instance it amounts to, "If you want to assimilate, do it; if you want to keep your heritage, do it." In either event, they are saying the people involved should be able to make the choice.

TABLE 8.1   *Views of Multiculturalism, Bilingualism,*
and Racial Discrimination, by Region (In %'s)

	Nationally	B.C.	Prairies	Ontario	Quebec	Atlantic
Multiculturalism						
Favour mosaic						
ideal	57	58	63	66	41	62
Favour melting pot	20	19	21	17	23	15
Bilingualism:						
Favour						
Teenagers	71	57	64	66	86	79
Adults*	55	44	36	51	83	38
Racial						
Discrimination						
Serious	57	53	56	54	64	52
Not serious	43	47	44	46	36	48

*Data Source: Project Can80.

One eighteen-year-old young woman from Montreal puts it this way:

> No, I don't see why these new immigrants should renounce their cultural differences, because there is nothing "duller" than the same kind of people all over. Why is it so interesting to visit Montreal? Because you see people of many nationalities and all kinds of things.

Bilingualism.   Canadian teenagers are more accepting of bilingualism than adult Canadians in every region of the country (see Table 8.1). Some 70% indicate that they favour the policy of bilingualism that Canada should have English and French as its two official languages. This compares, for example, with only 55% of adults surveyed in 1980–81, and 49% surveyed in 1975.[1]

Quebec teenagers are decisive about bilingualism. Contrary to the posture of their provincial government, they are almost unanimous (86%) in their support of Canada's two-language policy. Atlantic teenagers dramatically defy adult attitudes in their region, joining Quebec in solidly endorsing bilingualism. Commitment to two official languages declines gradually as one travels west of Quebec. The support level in Ontario is below the Atlantic provinces but is slightly higher than in western Canada. Nevertheless, Prairie teenagers depart significantly from Prairie adults in backing the two official languages policy. The lowest level of support for bilingualism is in B.C. Yet even there a majority (57%) endorse the policy.

Intergroup Attitudes

What are teenagers' feelings on the actual realization of the mosaic ideal? Slightly more than half of the country's teenagers believe that racial discrimination is a "very serious" or "fairly serious" national problem (see Table 8.1). Quebec teenagers, living in a province that historically has known considerable social disadvantage, are more likely than others to view racism as an issue. Yet, *the emerging generation gives evidence of being more accepting and less prejudiced than their parents and grandparents.*

French–English Relations. One in 10 teens see French–English relations as representing a "very serious" national problem, compared with 2 in 10 adults in both of the two surveys mentioned. Further, whereas 35% of adults outside Quebec indicated in the 1980–81 survey that French Canadians have "too much power" in the nation's affairs,[2] such perception is shared by 23% of teenagers outside Quebec. Similarly, 55% of Quebec adults felt that French Canadians have "too little power". In contrast, only 39% of Quebec teenagers share the same sentiments.

Still further, slightly more than 10% of either anglophones or francophones report that the other group is a target of jokes. This compares, for example, with some

20% for Ukrainians, 30% for Poles, and 50% for New-foundlanders. Both language categories see the other as highly friendly, intelligent, and clean (see Table 8.2). This is not to say, however, that there are no negative perception areas. Neither rates the other as highly when more subjective, integrity-related qualities are involved, namely, reliability and honesty. Here francophones are more wary of English Canadians than the reverse (see Table 8.2).

In short, French–English relations are improving over time. But there is still a distance to go.

Blacks.   Blacks appear to be something of "a favoured minority". Despite making up only one-tenth of 1% of Canada's population, 6 in 10 teens, as already noted, claim to be closely acquainted with one or more of them. Some 40% of young people see Blacks as having inadequate power in the nation's affairs. They exceed "the national average" in being viewed as friendly, reliable, honest, intelligent, and clean (see Table 8.2). While 3 in 10 teenagers indicate that Blacks are the subject of humour, in view of the positive stereotyping of many Black characteristics, there is good reason to believe that much of this humour is of a good-natured variety — as it is, for example, with Ukrainians, Poles, and Newfoundlanders. A grade twelve Saskatchewan male expresses it this way:

> Many students are prejudiced. But when a minority [member] is present who isn't a loser, he is generally accepted and on occasion, affectionately mocked.

Jews.   The 1983–84 publicity given "the Keegstra affair" in Alberta has suggested that anti-semitism is still prevalent in Canada. It will be recalled that a school teacher in a small community was accused of promoting hatred towards Jews in his classroom. Feeling pressure from the rest of the country, Alberta responded by establishing a task force to combat racism in the province.

The national survey has found that 1 in 3 teenagers are

TABLE 8.2 *Attitudes Towards Select Racial and Ethnic Groups* (In %'s)*

	Insuf. Power		Friendly	Reliable	Honest	Bright	Clean
	Teens	Adults*					
English Canadians — Francophones' view	15	17	72	30	32	57	54
French Canadians — Anglophones' view	21	21	77	40	43	45	59
Blacks	41	**	81	49	49	49	53
Jews	24	7	60	43	44	54	53
East Inds–Pakistanis	28	13	64	37	39	41	30
Canadian Indians	53	46	53	30	38	33	25
Average	30	21	70	38	41	47	46

*Data Source: Project Can80.
**No comparable 1980 data.

closely acquainted with one or more Jewish persons. While teenagers in Canada perceive Jews as having less power than English and French Canadians, they do see them as having more power than other racial minorities. Such a perception seems to reflect objective reality fairly accurately. Close to one-quarter feel that Jews have "too little power" in Canadian life, while only 9% say that they have "too much". In sharp contrast, only 7% of adults recently indicated that Jews have "too little power".[3] Compared with the national average, Jews are seen as being somewhat less friendly, yet slightly more reliable, honest, intelligent, and clean than others (see Table 8.2). Further, Jews are viewed as the subject of humour by about 1 in 5 teens.

TABLE 8.3   *Perception of Valued Traits Among Jews,*
              by Region (In %'s)

	Nationally	B.C.	Prairies	Ontario	Quebec	Atlantic
Friendly	60	67	70	61	48	61
Hard working	59	63	65	63	48	59
Clean	53	59	60	57	39	54
Intelligent	54	50	56	57	51	49
Polite	47	58	58	47	35	53
Honest	44	50	54	45	28	53
Reliable	43	50	55	45	27	47
Caring	42	53	49	41	34	47

Our knowledge of the content of some of that humour
leads us to suggest that Jewish jokes tend to be derogatory,
rather than — as with Blacks and some other groups —
somewhat playful.

Contrary to the deduction many Canadians have made
in the light of the Keegstra incident, negative views of
Jews are considerably less common in Western Canada
than in Ontario, and especially in Quebec. A majority of
young people in Quebec are highly reluctant to assign
valued characteristics to Jews. Teenagers in Ontario and
Quebec are consistently less inclined than their Western
and Atlantic counterparts to associate positive characteristics with Jews (see Table 8.3). This is not so much the case
with "objective traits" that are difficult to deny, such as
intelligence, industry, and friendliness. But the generalization does hold for more "subjective" character assessments,
relating to qualities such as honesty, reliability, and caring.

East Indians and Pakistanis.   Even though East Indians
and Pakistanis do not have significant influence and power
in Canadian life, in the minds of most teenagers they do
not need more power. In other words, most teenagers
believe no power is enough power for East Indians and
Pakistanis in Canada. Teenagers' perceptions of sufficient

power for this category increase consistently as one moves westward, from 25% in the Atlantic region through 33% in Ontario to 44% in B.C. Yet, even so, young people differ dramatically from adults. While 28% of teens feel East Indians and Pakistanis do not have enough power, this is double the comparable 1980–81 13% figure for adults.

In the course of having close contact with one in three teenagers, East Indians and Pakistanis are commonly associated with a number of socially undesirable stereotypes. Like Jews, they are viewed by many as somewhat unfriendly. However, unlike Jews, they tend to be seen by only *a minority* as reliable, honest, intelligent, and clean (see Table 8.2). Further, more than 30% of Canadian young people point out that East Indians and Pakistanis are the subjects of humour. As with Jews, it appears that much of this humour is of a very negative variety.

Canadian Indians. Although Jews are approximately as numerous as native Indians (1.5%) and typically more socially accessible, more than 40% of young people assert that they have close contact with Indians, compared with slightly more than 30% for Jews. The stereotypes concerning Indians, in part supposedly informed by that contact, are somewhat paradoxical.

On the one hand, some 53% of teenagers — compared with 46% of adults — feel that Canadian Indians do not have enough power in Canadian affairs. However, Indians receive the lowest assignment of valued traits of any cultural minority considered. Barely one-half characterize them as friendly, and only 1 in 3 feel that they tend to be reliable, honest, intelligent, or clean. At the same time, Canadian Indians are fairly infrequently a target of humour; just 7% say that native Indians are featured "when people [they] know tell jokes".

It would seem that young people typically have limited hostility towards Indians, viewing them with negative imagery while at the same time believing they deserve a better fate in Canadian life.

Some Other Groups.   Additional limited information was gathered on other cultural minorities. More than 5 in 10 teenagers say that they have close contact with Orientals, a higher figure than for ties with Canadian Indians, Jews, and East Indians–Pakistanis, even though Orientals are outnumbered by all of those groups. The perception of the power of Orientals in Canadian life is virtually identical to that of Jews and East Indians–Pakistanis (9% "too much", 27% "too little"). Correspondingly, Orientals are seen as having more power than Blacks and Canadian Indians. As with native Indians, they are not a major target of teenage humour (8%). Thus, Orientals, like Blacks, appear to be one of Canada's "favoured minorities".

Attitudes towards some other groups were explored through asking the extent to which those groups are featured in the jokes told by people teenagers know. About 50% cite Newfoundlanders, 25% Poles, and 15% Ukrainians. As would be expected, "Newfy" jokes are most popular in the Atlantic region, Ontario, and, to a lesser extent, Quebec. Polish-directed humour has its greatest following in B.C., while Ukrainian jokes are most common on the Prairies.

This humour, as with much of humour focused on Blacks, appears to be fairly light and non-vicious, similar in "softness" to traditional jokes starring frugal Scotsmen. Nonetheless, at minimum, it does reflect power relations: the jokes feature less powerful economic and cultural minorities. The opening line of a typical regional or cultural joke — "How many Newfies does it take to screw in a light bulb?" — would get little response when rephrased, "How many Ontarians . . . "

Importance of National Group Background

Survey researchers typically ask people for their parents' ancestry and then proceed to churn out tables analysing differences in attitudes and behaviour by one's "ethnicity".

Such observers as the late John Porter of Carleton University have been highly critical of such procedures.[4] They maintain that we may well be "spinning statistical fiction", creating ethnic identifications that in fact are largely nonexistent. As a result, such "fictitious" national heritages typically are found by researchers to have inconsequential effects on thought and action.

Aware of such a critique, we asked Canadian teenagers, "How important do you consider your national cultural group background (such as English, French, Italian, German) to be?" We found that only 25% of teenagers regard their "background group" as "very important". About 55% say that is is "somewhat important", while 20% indicate that it is "not very important". National background appears to be highly important for more than 50% of teenagers with Italian, Greek, Portuguese, and Oriental histories. It also seems to be very important for about 25% of young people of English, Dutch, German, Polish, and Ukrainian descent. Conspicuous by their absence are teenagers of French ancestry; just under 20% indicate that their French or French Canadian background is "very important" to them.

These findings invariably raise the age-old Canadian question: Is someone first a Canadian, or first committed to some other country or ethnic heritage? One of our teenage respondents expresses this common attitude:

> Although I support the idea of a "mosaic", I wish there was more of a feeling of Canadian identity among people of different races. I think that within the mosaic, people consider themselves firstly as [related to their] native countries and then as a Canadian.

We did not ask teenagers to make such loyalty choices. However, in addition to probing the importance of their family histories, we did explore the issue of the value they place on being a Canadian.

Specifically, we asked them how important "being a

Canadian" is to them. About 50% maintain that it is "very important". This compares with about 25% who say the same for their parental background. And we found that, contrary to popular belief, young people who most highly value their national heritages are far more inclined *also* to highly value being a Canadian (61%) than are teenagers who place little value on their ethnic backgrounds (35%).

What these results suggest is that there is seldom such a thing as a "hyphenated Canadian". Rather there are what we might call "single focus" nationalists and "double focus" nationalists. There are Canadians who appreciate their country while being indifferent to their ethnic origins, and there are Canadians who are bonded to Canada while at the same time being attached to their historical roots in another country. Canadians who have resented "the immigrant invasion" should take special note. In the majority of cases, the offspring of immigrants who retain strong sentiments about their previous country are among the most patriotic Canadians.

Social Attitudes

Again reflecting the socialization "success" of our major institutions, Canadian teenagers exhibit a strong tendency to endorse "the status quo". Young people — even more so than adults — consistently exhibit belief in the fairness of "the system". They are more inclined, for example, to maintain that hard work enables people to succeed and that the police treat lawbreakers fairly (see Table 8.4). Teenagers are also just as likely as adults to *oppose* the legalization of marijuana. They reflect a slightly more pro-person attitude in being *less likely* to favour capital punishment and exhibit the same level of "social compassion" as adults concerning the poor having a right to medical care and at least a subsistence income. Also, despite the alleged impact

TABLE 8.4 *Attitudes Towards Social Issues: Teenagers and Adults* (% Agreeing)*

	Teens	Adults
Anyone who works hard will rise to the top	74	44
The police treat lawbreakers equally regardless of age, race, or sex	51	38
The use of marijuana should be legalized	28	28
The death penalty should sometimes be used to punish criminals	73	83
People who cannot afford it have a right to medical care	94	96
People who are poor have a right to an income adequate to live on	91	87
Married women should not work if their husbands are capable of supporting them	17	28
Women should take care of running their homes and leave running of the country up to men	12	15
The average Canadian does not have any influence on what the government does	64	52
Clergy should stick to religion and not concern themselves with economic and political problems	50	41

*Data Source: Project Can80.

of the feminist movement, today's teenagers are only slightly less traditional in their views regarding women either working or being involved in politics.

However, as the next section shows, it is possible to isolate a scepticism about institutions; teenagers are somewhat more negative than adults about the possibility of average people influencing government decisions. They are also slightly more inclined than adults to assert that clergy should not get embroiled in social issues. As emphasized in Chapter One, the emerging generation gives little evidence of wanting to lead the nation into revolution.

Attitudes Towards Major Institutions

We asked teenagers, "How much confidence do you have in the people in charge . . ." of a variety of institutions. The greatest amount of confidence is shown in the police (77%)—suggesting, we maintain, the faith teenagers have in "the goodness and fairness" of the system (see Table 8.5). The placement of police at the top of the confidence ladder is intriguing. Police forces have included a service role as part of their function. They visit schools regularly and speak on various subjects. Their cars are signed with slogans such as "To Serve and Protect". It appears that young people have decided to place their confidence in the police because they have computed that the police are out for their well-being.

At a second level of institutional representatives receiving teenagers' confidence are those in charge of schools, churches, the court system, and science (around 65% each). The media — newspapers and television leaders specifically — receive a third level of teenage confidence (some 50%). Government, whether federal or provincial, forms a fourth-level category of confidence (about 40%). Labour union leaders register lowest on the confidence scale (35%).

Criticisms of government are of the fairly predictable variety. From a Toronto grade twelve male comes this comment:

> I believe the government spends too much money on investigations and trips, instead of reinvesting it in Canada and creating jobs.

A seventeen-year-old female living in a small B.C. town complains:

> The government shouldn't waste so much money when it could be used wisely. The politicians need to realize the need of farmers because they are the backbones of the country.

And from a small southern Ontario community comes the observation of a female in grade twelve:

> My hopes and dreams for the future are rapidly being destroyed by the lack of confidence I have in the leaders of the Western World (i.e., Ronald Reagan, Pierre Trudeau, Brian Mulroney, etc.).

Regional variations in confidence are fairly minor. Quebec teenagers tend to express more confidence than others in virtually all leaders, with the exception of the police and the churches. They also indicate more confidence in federal than in provincial government leaders. B.C. young people generally are slightly more critical than others. And Atlantic teenagers, reflecting their relatively higher level of religious commitment, are more positive about churches than their counterparts elsewhere.

In a related finding, teenagers tend to see politicians,

TABLE 8.5 *Confidence in Institution Leaders, by Region*

% Indicating "A Great Deal" or "Quite a Bit"

	Nationally	B.C.	Prairies	Ontario	Quebec	Atlantic
The police	77	74	81	78	72	80
The schools	68	57	68	67	74	69
The court system	67	63	67	62	71	72
Science	65	62	61	57	79	63
The churches	62	50	64	62	61	73
Television	57	53	54	50	69	54
Newspapers	48	43	50	45	54	44
Your provincial govt.	40	29	44	40	41	38
The federal govt.	39	30	35	38	47	38
Labour unions	35	30	30	32	44	36

the media, and labour unions as having "too much power" in the country's affairs. Reflecting the ideal of egalitarianism in national influence, they single out rich people, corporations, Americans, and, to a lesser extent, men as also having excessive power. As with institutional confidence, Quebec teenagers are not as critical as others of politicians, the media, labour unions, or big corporations. Atlantic young people are also more favourable in their responses about union power than other teenagers. However, they are more negative than other teenagers about the influence of rich people and the big corporations.

A seventeen-year-old female from a small coastline town in B.C. offers what we regard as an extremely insightful observation on different levels of power:

> The amount of power these groups have is hard to say, but they only have too much power if they use it for their own benefit and not for the benefit of all the people of the world.

Perception of the Major Social Issues

An important qualification about these perceptions must be made. Since few people, if any, ever personally experience the scope of every potential social issue, the perception of what represents a serious social problem will be largely the product of social sources, immediate experience, and personal characteristics.

Accordingly, Canadian young people would be expected to "see" as "critical social problems" those issues "popularized" in the culture through the activities of the various institutions, including the media. They would also be expected to "see" local conditions as constituting "national" problems. Finally, depending on their own features — values, beliefs, and attitudes — some issues would be "seen" as more serious than others.[5]

The Immediate Issues

Such patterns are readily apparent in the survey findings. Reflecting publicity and experience, unemployment is singled out as the number one social problem in every region of the country (see Table 8.6). Media, immediate environment, and personal values seem to be interacting in leading 40–50% to view the threat of nuclear war, along with "individual centred issues" — child abuse, crime, drugs, sexual assault, alcoholism, and teenage suicide — as extremely serious problems.

Each of these issues has been given extensive media coverage in recent times. *Child abuse*, physically, sexually, and emotionally, is currently a widely-publicized topic. Its profile was raised significantly during 1984 through the release of the report of the federal Committee on Sexual Offences Against Children and Youths, headed by Robin Badgley of the University of Toronto.[6] The study suggests that 1 in 2 females and 1 in 3 males have been victims of unwanted sexual acts, ranging from fondling to intercourse. The finding that 4 in 5 of the incidents happened in childhood or adolescent years makes the perception that child abuse is a significant problem more than a theoretical statement for many of the teenagers who participated in our survey. The attention being given the topic by professionals can be seen in the response to the Fifth International Congress on Child Abuse and Neglect, held in Montreal in September 1984. The three-day conference attracted more than 2,000 doctors, social workers, psychologists, psychiatrists, and others from 42 countries.[7]

The possibility of *nuclear annihilation* is something the emerging generation has never lived without. They were born into a world engaged in a nuclear arms race and have heard the disarmament debates for as long as they can remember. In 1984 they watched *The Day After* on television with the rest of the country, witnessing what many of them feel is a simulation of the imminent real thing. Some researchers, including Patricia Blackwell and John Gessner of Loyola University in New Orleans, maintain that living in a nuclear age has significant consequences for adolescents. Young people who are already experiencing the traumatic crises of adolescence also have to accept uncertainty about the future, thus living for the moment and not infrequently experiencing extreme tension, anxiety, and depression.[8] The comments of our survey respondents illuminate their mood. A Nova Scotia sixteen-year-old says with intensity:

> We must do something about nuclear weapons and the threat of nuclear war. We, the young Canadians, want to have a future to look forward to without the threat of war. I can't express how important this is.

From the interior of British Columbia comes this observation from a fifteen-year-old female:

> Nuclear war is the worst problem in the world today. It should be the foremost object of concern!

And a grade ten Ontario student expresses her concern this way:

> Well, for one thing, it's inevitable. Do you realize that everyone in the world could die within the next half hour? If there is a "World War III", I don't think we will live to see the end of it.

The results of a November 1984 survey of 1,000 Metropolitan Toronto high-school students reinforce our findings. Some 51% of the participating students rated nuclear war among their three top fears, slightly above the fear of unemployment. Sixty-three percent reported some feelings of anxiety about war, and 10% said they thought about it daily. However, 90% believed that nothing they did would be effective in preventing nuclear war.[9] In December 1984, students at the University of Victoria were petitioned to hold a referendum on mass suicide in the event of nuclear attack and a call for the university's health services centre to stock suicide pills. Not surprisingly, today's young people have been called "The Pessimistic Generation".[10]

To varying degrees, Canada's teenagers have first-hand experience with other realities regarded by them as very serious: crime, alcoholism, and suicide. But there are few issues that have received more public attention than *drugs*. Some 50% of Canadian adults see drug abuse as a "very serious" problem, while another 35% view it as a "fairly serious" problem.[11] They typically have young people in mind.

Interestingly, the survey has found that about 50% of Canadian teenagers *also* think that drug use constitutes a "very serious" national problem — only unemployment is viewed as appreciably more serious. Alcoholism is seen by 40% as a severe problem. Further, 68% are opposed to the legalization of the use of a popular drug such as marijuana. Nevertheless, about 30% admit to using drugs, with some 5% saying they do so very often, 12% sometimes, and 13% seldom. This 30% national figure for drug use is at least partly corroborated by a 1981 study of Ontario high-school students, which found that 30% had used marijuana in the previous year.[12]

Approximately 60%, however, claim to be fairly regular users of alcohol. To some this might sound high, but it is very similar to the 56% figure the national Canadian Health Survey found in 1979.[13] It appears that an additional 20% of teenagers imbibe on certain occasions.

Further, around 30% are regular cigarette smokers, while another 10% smoke once in a while. These figures also are similar to those found by other researchers.[14] Generally speaking, acknowledged illicit drug, alcohol, and tobacco use varies little by either region of the country or gender. Illegal drugs are consumed somewhat more in B.C. (40%) than elsewhere (some 30%), and more by males (33%)

than females (28%). However, differences by region for both alcohol and tobacco use among adolescents are statistically insignificant.

It appears that at least four major motives are involved in teenage drug use.[15] The majority try drugs out of curiosity, to see what they are like. A second motive is enjoyment. Ronald Clavier, a psychologist with the Clarke

---

TABLE 8.6   *Perception of Social Problems by Region (In %'s)*

	% Indicating Issues Are "Very Serious" Problems					
	Nationally	*B.C.*	*Prairies*	*Ontario*	*Quebec*	*Atlantic*
Unemployment	61	71	56	54	67	67
Child abuse	50	51	48	51	50	49
Crime	48	46	45	47	53	49
Threat of nuclear war	48	49	44	49	49	49
Drugs	46	43	41	46	48	55
Sexual assault	46	43	45	47	46	43
Alcoholism	41	39	37	41	40	53
Suicide	41	36	38	38	50	42
The economy	37	45	38	33	37	40
Pollution	37	25	25	36	52	32
Poverty	33	31	28	31	38	34
Juvenile delinquency	29	28	24	28	34	33
Divorce	23	16	20	24	28	19
Racial discrimination	22	23	20	23	24	20
Unequal treat. women	15	15	13	14	18	17
Lack of Canadian unity	13	15	10	12	14	13
French–Eng. relations	13	9	9	10	20	12

Institute of Psychiatry in Toronto, told a 1984 Addiction Awareness Week seminar in Ontario that "school children take drugs because it's fun."[16] Social pressure is a third factor. One Saskatchewan male respondent expresses it this way:

> I feel that the older generation of Canadians don't understand the pressure that the younger generation faces concerning such areas as sex, drugs, and alcohol. Many parents grew up in a time when drug abuse wasn't a problem, and they don't understand the peer pressure involved.

A fourth motive is escape: trying drugs to relieve tensions, anxieties, and pressures. From a mountain community in B.C. comes this poignant observation:

> Today's teenagers have many pressures on them. Some handle the pressures well. Some turn to drugs to help. My best friend died four years ago because she thought she couldn't make it without drugs.

A graduating female adds:

> I feel that today's teenagers are under much more pressure to grow up and attain a responsible position in society. These pressures overcome some, and for moments they turn to alcohol or drugs. I think we are being forced from diapers to three-piece suits — no time for fun.

The Abstract Issues

Broader societal issues appear to be somewhat more difficult for the average teenager to grasp. Thus it is that such apparently obvious, "objectively serious" problems as the economy, pollution, and poverty are not so perceived by a majority of young people. If media attention on a particular issue is not combined with immediate experience and a measure of personal concern, the issue is not likely to be translated into a serious social problem. As a result, whether or not areas such as the inequality of women and the lack of Canadian unity are "objectively" serious or not, they are only perceived as urgent problems by a small minority of the country's youth.

Indicative of "the levelling effect" of media and other forms of socialization is the remarkable consistency of problem perception across the regions of the country. Variations are far less striking than the overall pattern of similarity.

Assessment

The survey findings show that our institutions have experienced considerable success in instilling ideals concerning the rights and characteristics of other Canadians. Canadian teenagers, at this stage of their lives, have more contact with a wider variety of the people in this country than do their parents. And whereas their parents and grandparents have commonly resented the efforts of the federal government to introduce and formalize the twin policies of bilingualism and multiculturalism, young people are showing receptivity to both ideals.

Even more, whereas their adult predecessors have often held negative and, indeed, hostile attitudes towards new Canadians, including non-Whites, today's teenager is exhibiting less resistance to such minorities. In addition to the percentage responses to items given, comments such as the following are encouraging:

> I believe in judging people as individuals, not as members of ethnic groups.
>
> — grade twelve female, St. John's, Newfoundland

> A person's race and how he acts have *no* common denominators. You could meet a nice Indian or a rotten Anglo.
>
> — grade eleven male, Montreal

I think that all people, whether they are Jewish, black, or Oriental, etc., possess all [desirable] qualities. It is our duty as a society to allow these qualities to be brought out in individuals so that they can contribute to the world in which we live.

— grade twelve female, eastern Alberta

This is not to say that undesirable stereotypes have disappeared. On the contrary, they are highly prevalent, notably in the cases of Canadian Indians along with East Indians and Pakistanis. It is therefore important to take ongoing readings of intergroup relations and pursue means of alleviating problems — as the Alberta government has done with its 1984 Committee on Tolerance and Understanding, provoked by the Keegstra incident. The committee has suggested, for example, that teachers need to be better prepared to cope with children from diverse cultures. Committee chairman Ron Ghitter has stated that teachers "are ill-equipped" and that "if we're going to have intercultural education, the teachers have to have the tools."[17]

Yet, compared with Canadian adults, the attitudes of teenagers — if reflected in behaviour in the present and future — appear to offer hope for improved intergroup relations in this country.

Our institutions have also "succeeded" in inculcating dominant adult social attitudes. Most young people endorse the political, economic, legal, and gender status quo. What criticisms they do make, as in their reservations about labour and government, rich people and corporations, and, to a lesser degree, the media, seem also to be largely *learned*. In a capitalistic democracy, government and the excessively rich at the one extreme, labour at the other, and the media as the commentators — all these are "fair game" for the onlooker. Such a right to dissent is an anticipated part of the system, rather than necessarily a reflective response to it.

Former University of Alberta sociologist Gwynn Nettler has observed that the two foremost concerns of the world's people are to stay alive and to live well.[18] These two central concerns are also apparent in the case of Canadian teenagers. Their major worries — nuclear war, crime, child abuse, sexual assault — pertain to "staying alive" issues. Employment further makes it possible not only to live, but also to "live well". Once these basic problems are overcome, it becomes possible to turn to "more extravagant" social issues: uniting a country, pollution, discrimination, poverty.

As with values, sexual attitudes, and beliefs, the views teenagers have of people and the world are shaped by adult institutions. Emergence into adulthood produces at least two critical problems related to such imparted views of the world. The first pertains to *participation*. As teenagers emerge, they increasingly want to have the opportunity not only to influence their own lives, but also to influence what is happening in the world around them. Some are very vocal. A grade twelve male from a small Newfoundland town comments:

> For some reason, teenagers are always overlooked. Many of us are capable of making intelligent decisions on matters affecting us, but no one ever asks us. I am tired of taking a back seat on things that concern me.

From a private school in B.C., a sixteen-year-old male says:

> We are willing to contribute responsibly to our society, but there is no avenue.

An eighteen-year-old Montreal CEGEP (Collèges d'Enseignement Général Et Professionel) student notes:

> Adults always say that the young are the future, but they also are the present!

Another B.C. teenager, a grade eleven female from Vancouver, expresses exasperation with the powerlessness of teenagers:

It is frustrating at times to watch adults change our futures by creating bombs, changing school systems, fluctuating the economy, and changing diplomatic relations. The bomb question has many sides, and I have not been able to decide anything except that I fear its power. The school and the economy will affect my life, and those I wish I could change now.

A rural Ontario grade ten student states the problem succinctly:

I think Canadian young people have more to offer this country than you give us credit for. Give us a chance!

Sociologist Frank Fasick of the University of Waterloo has carefully examined the relationship between the biological development of adolescents and minimum age legislation in Canada. He notes that socially defined adolescence "extends well beyond the point at which most young persons attain full sexual and intellectual powers, as well as the bulk of their overall physical growth".[19]

Consequently, the failure of our society as a whole to take the contributions of "adolescents" seriously means that many capable young people under the age of eighteen are allowed to give little significant input. For some teenagers, such a negation of what they feel they are becoming is dehumanizing. For society, it appears to represent the loss of a potentially valuable resource.

A second problem associated with emergence and the "successful" instilling of ideas pertains to *disparity between the ideal and the real*. Institutions tend to transmit what should be rather than what is when promoting values and attitudes. Humanitarianism, for example, is "in". Teachers, parents, journalists, TV commentators, disc jockeys, coaches, and preachers are among the multitude who officially endorse it. The topic can be anything from the mistreatment of Russian Jews to a telethon for muscular dystrophy to the local United Way campaign. Everyone cares.

In practice, of course, most of us are not quite so caring in dealing with ordinary people in everyday settings. The student who helps wrap the classroom Christmas hamper can be forgiven, or perhaps applauded, for quietly wondering why his teacher, who is spearheading the project, does not seem to like him.

As teenagers emerge, encountering the world "as it really is", the potential for disenchantment is obvious. How one subsequently responds both to that world and its institutions depends largely on the fate of one's hopes and expectations. We now proceed to an examination of those dreams and plans.

9

HOPES AND EXPECTATIONS

How Teenagers View the Future

*Teenagers today are scared. With
unemployment, the economy, divorce and
the world's peace situation — we all wonder
what will happen.*
— a sixteen-year-old female from rural Quebec

Living the teenage years in our society is like driving in
heavy traffic without knowing where you want to go or
whether you will be able to get there. In addition to many
quandaries about themselves, teenagers are increasingly
feeling puzzled about a world that is extremely complex.
They are bombarded with expectations from parents, teachers, ministers, advertisers, the media, and their friends. As
they stand in the midst of the traffic, they are forced not
only to dream but to plan. With plans come hopes, and
with hopes, expectations.

The Canadian Dream

While often overshadowed by the American dream of pro-
gressing from "log cabin to White House", there is also a

pervasive Canadian Dream. It is learned in childhood and is the product of our central institutions: the school, the media, the family, the church, the government and, of course, the business community. Teenagers have taken in with mother's milk the views: "This is a land of opportunity. Education will open doors for you. Individual excellence will be rewarded. Work hard and you will be successful. The best, after all, eventually arrive at the top, and enjoy the good life."

Lands of opportunity make promises and breed optimism. As noted in the previous chapter, some 70% of teenagers agree with the ideal that "anyone who works hard will rise to the top." One grade twelve female from a small southern Ontario town proclaims:

> At our age we can do anything and be whoever we want to be if we want it bad enough.

Interestingly, many adults who have had to wrestle with the ideal have modified their expectations. Only 44% of them still concur with such an idea. Their disillusionment is readily apparent.

One message society transmits to young people is that the good life requires an education. When asked "What do you plan to do after high school?" about 75% indicated that they want to go on for further education (see Table 9.1).

Although less than 20% of the parents of the teenagers surveyed have university degrees themselves, the big teen dream is to go to university. When teenagers are fifteen years old, almost 65% of them plan to experience life on campus (see Table 9.1). However, by the time those same teenagers are nineteen, less than 40% still see themselves as university-bound. Over a period of four years, the dream of a university education dissolves for more than half of Canadian teenagers. By the time registration lines form on campus, the numbers have been cut in half again. Only about 15% of all high-school students — under 1 in 7 — actually attend university following graduation from high

TABLE 9.1 *Plans After High School by Region, Gender, and Age (In %'s)*

"What do you plan to do after high school?"

	Try Get a Job	Go to Univ.	Go to Tech–Bus.	Other	Un-decided	Totals
Nationally	16	54	23	3	4	100
British Columbia	16	47	28	3	6	100
Prairies	18	48	24	5	5	100
Ontario	15	61	17	3	4	100
Quebec	15	50	28	3	4	100
Atlantic	15	58	19	5	3	100
Males	17	51	25	4	3	100
Females	14	57	21	3	5	100
15	10	63	22	2	3	100
16	13	53	25	4	5	100
17	17	53	21	5	4	100
18	23	51	20	2	4	100
19	33	37	21	1	8	100

school. Most teenagers taste the pain of relinquishing their university education dream before they turn twenty.

As the number of young people intending to go to university declines, the number planning to try to get a job increases. At least two factors seem to be involved. Contrary to societal propaganda and parental hopes, a university education is still beyond the financial means of many. Further, given the state of the economy, university degrees are seen as having dubious value if the primary objective is to qualify for a job.

In 1983 government sources claimed that 26% of young people between the ages of fifteen and twenty-four were enrolled in post-secondary institutions in Canada. It thus appears that approximately one-third of those young people who hope to continue their education past high school actually realize their intentions.

Regional variations in post-high-school plans are minor. Teenagers in Ontario and the Atlantic region are slightly more likely than others to look to university rather than technical or business post-secondary institutions.

Perhaps reflecting the fact that females now believe that a wide range of occupations is available to them, a slightly higher proportion of young women than young men indicate that they plan to go to university; relatedly, males are somewhat more apt to see their post-high-school lives involving a job or a technical or business-school training (see Table 9.1).

Life Beyond School

The question of what young people will do after they finish their education has already been cited in Chapter Four as their most pressing personal concern. Only 1 in 10 teenagers say they are not troubled significantly by the issue. This concern among teenagers is pervasive in all regions of Canada at all ages and characterizes males and females equally. The paramount question for teenagers is the "life-after question", not with respect to death but to school.

As a means of probing teenagers' plans beyond the classroom, we asked:

> When you finish your education do you plan to:
> 1 Get a job, and eventually marry
> 2 Get a job, but not marry
> 3 Get married, and not work outside the home
> 4 Get married, but also work outside the home

While options 1 and 4 appear to be quite similar, they were carefully designed to explore the respondents' emphasis. For those teenagers planning to combine the roles, option 1 is weighted towards one's career, while the fourth choice emphasizes the marriage side.

About 7 in 10 say they intend to get a job and eventually marry, while only 1 in 10 emphasize getting married but also working outside the home (see Table 9.2). Most of the remainder indicate they plan to get a job but not marry. And only 1% say that they plan to get married and not work outside the home.

An analysis by region reveals considerable consistency throughout the country, with the exception of Quebec. One in 4 teenagers in that province indicate that they intend to work but stay single, compared with only 10% in other regions.

Perhaps somewhat surprisingly, only 1% of female teenagers say they intend to marry and not work outside the home. If translated into behaviour, such plans would represent a major change from the current situation. Currently only about 50% of all women work for pay, with 60% of these women married, 30% single, and 10% widowed, separated, or divorced.[2] Among them are 58% of the mothers of the teenagers in our survey. Regardless of

---

TABLE 9.2   *Plans After Education by Region, Gender, and Age (In %'s)*

"When you finish your education, do you plan to:"

	Get Job, Event. Marry	Get Job, Not Marry	Marry, Not Wk Out Hm	Marry, Work Out Hm	Totals
Nationally	72	15	1	12	100
British Columbia	77	10	0	13	100
Prairies	78	10	1	11	100
Ontario	75	11	1	13	100
Quebec	62	26	2	10	100
Atlantic	77	11	1	11	100
Males	77	16	1	6	100
Females	68	14	1	17	100

the values one places on such possible imminent change, the implications for the size of the work force and the problem of unemployment are somewhat staggering.

It is also interesting to recall a relevant finding from the previous chapter, that 17% of teens feel that "married women should not work if their husbands are capable of supporting them." About 20% of males are in agreement with this position, compared with only 5% of females. And the young women who plan to work are adamant. Some 95% of the females who envision having a career without marriage disagree with such traditionalism, as do 95% of the females who, personally, plan to marry. Something, it would appear, is going to have to give. . .

Employment

Until recent years, there was a Canadian assumption that jobs are available to those who want to work. The availability of employment was almost treated as a basic "human right". Recent recession, technological advances, a work force that includes more women, and the inability of governments individually and collectively to control the economy have all forced us to surrender this assumption.

Canadian young people have witnessed the impact of declining school enrolments in their everyday lives. They read in the newspaper that school boards are being forced to release an annual quota of teachers. They say goodbye to teachers who will not be returning in the fall. They sense the trauma in others, and feel the loss themselves. They notice that the average age of high-school teachers in increasing.

Teenagers go to movies and watch robots like "R2D2" perform impressive feats and quickly compute that robots are more efficient than people for many jobs both now and in the future. Listening to the news before supper, they hear that 300 graduating lawyers and 1,350 new engineers face "no vacancy" signs in their respective professions. Mentally they cross two further vocational options off their lists. They remember well how they wanted to work last summer, but only found a job that paid the minimum wage and lasted for just two weeks.

Young people are worried. Society's economic promises are in danger of being unfulfilled. Little wonder that, in needing some institutional source to blame, teenagers are critical of government. Aware of the plight of many about to graduate and seeing the employment problem ahead for himself, an Alberta sixteen-year-old laments:

> [Teenagers] go to school for twelve years and when they get out of school they have to fight for work, and if they don't get work they get labelled as young punks or lazy bums. It isn't their fault they can't find work. The government isn't helping them any.

Increasing economic and social strain seems inevitable. And this strain will only be intensified by present high expectations. On the one hand, teenagers recognize the potential employment problem. They acknowledge with one sixteen-year-old from the Okanagan that

> with or without education jobs are scarce because of the economy.

On the other hand, while they perceive unemployment as a severe problem, they continue to have a remarkable amount of optimism about their *own personal* employment prospects. More than 70% maintain that when they complete their education, they "think that [they] will be able to find a good job". Optimism about future employment varies only slightly by region. These variations reflect actual employment conditions in being somewhat higher in Ontario, Quebec, and the Prairies, and slightly lower in B.C. and the Atlantic regions. There is little difference in employment optimism by either age or, significantly, *gender*. Female teenagers have as high employment hopes as males. Only a minority share the realism expressed by a Charlottetown grade eleven female:

I might have the job requirements but the jobs might not be there.

Even fewer admit to the extreme pessimism of a Newfoundland grade ten student:

> There won't be any jobs around. If older people who are more qualified can't find jobs, how can I?

Marriage

There has been considerable speculation in recent decades about the future of conventional marriage. A recent survey by Family Services of America has projected that by the year 2000 there will be a drop in the percentage of North Americans who marry — to 85% from 90%. The Family Services report attributes such a decline to "weakening religious, social and legal taboos, greater sexual freedom promoting continued growth of cohabitation, single-person households, unwed single-parent families, and homosexual couples."[3]

Our survey findings, however, do not point to such a decline. While at this point in time 85% of teenagers say they plan to marry, it seems sound to assert that this is a minimum figure. Many will undoubtedly marry who, in their late teens, are not envisioning doing so. Whatever they are observing abut the present state of marriage and divorce in our society, most teenagers still believe that their desire to be loved can best be fulfilled in a marital relationship. We are not alone in our assertion. American family researchers Flake-Hobson, Robinson, and Skeen write, "Adolescents do not agree with the idea that 'marriage is out of date' and most eventually plan to marry and have children."[4]

Their comment about children holds for Canada. More than 50% of the teenagers in our sample indicate that they would like to have two children, while 20% envision having three. About 15% would like four or more children, while the remainder want either only one child (7%) or none at all (8%).

A highly significant pattern that thus emerges concerning "life beyond school" is the similarity of expectations for females and males. The national survey reveals that Canadian teenage females presently differ very little from their male counterparts in planning to attend university and have a career, while also marrying and having children. This would seem to represent a very important change from past gender expectations. Accordingly, it is now precarious to assert, as did status of women advisory council representatives meeting in Quebec in late 1984, that the "women's movement has had little impact on adolescent girls who believe love and marriage are more important than education and a good job."[5] Reality notwithstanding, males and females share very similar expectations.

Teenage Dreams

Optimism in teenagers is a breeding ground for their dreams. Recognizing that adolescents are at least beginning to chart their adult futures in their minds, we asked them to share some of their hopes and expectations. They did so by responding to a series of "If . . ." statements.

"If I Could be Anyone . . ."   A sizeable proportion, 3 in 10, indicate that they would simply "like to be me". They appear to have healthy self-concepts and are approaching life positive about who they are.

Another 2 in 10 teenagers say they identify with stars in the entertainment and sports worlds. If cloning were an option, many would like to be a Wayne Gretzky, a Carling Bassett, or a Michael Jackson. As would be expected, another 2 in 10 find appealing the scenario of being rich and successful. The prospect of "living well", complete with a luxurious home, expensive cars, and an unlimited cash-flow captures their dreams. A further 1 in 10 have varied hopes and fantasies. They see themselves, for example, as heads of state, famous writers, and Nobel Prize winners.

If there is a segment to be concerned about, it is the remaining 2 in 10 who have no personal dreams. Many, on the surface at least, appear to lack imagination and perhaps optimism. Without dreams there are no goals or hopes. Fortunately, for them and society, they form a minority.

"If I Could Live in Any Country . . ."   Teenagers in our society are pro-Canadian. We have already seen that more than 50% regard "being a Canadian" as very important. Another 30% say that it is "somewhat important" to them. Given the hypothetical opportunity of living in any country, more than 60% say that they would choose Canada. In the words of one southern Ontario seventeen-year-old:

> I am *proud* to be a Canadian because our country has done many great things. I don't think I would ever want to live anywhere else.

The influence and appeal of the U.S. is also evident. Approximately 15% of Canadian teenagers would prefer to move south. As one fifteen-year-old male from Quebec puts it:

> I love Canada but the U.S.A. offers better opportunities for jobs, and the cost of living is cheaper.

The remaining 25% would exercise various options. Australia has come to have some mystique; 5% would like to live "down under". English and French cultural roots do not hold as much appeal. Only 3% wish they could live in England or France. An equal proportion would like to move to Switzerland.

If I Could Live in Any Province. . ."   There is considerable unrest among teenagers regarding their preference of which province to live in. Whether the choice is to remain in the province where they presently live or to move to another part of Canada, the appeal of "Beautiful British Columbia" is unchallenged. Almost 80% of teens living in B.C. would like to remain right where they are. A slight majority of teenagers in Alberta, Ontario, Quebec, and the three Maritime provinces would prefer to remain in their present provinces (see Table 9.3).

Teenagers who want to move tend to look to B.C. It is the first choice of mobile-minded young people in every province except Prince Edward Island and Quebec, in which cases the preference is Ontario. Generally speaking, Ontario and Alberta are the next two choices of teenagers who want to leave their provinces. At the "low appeal" extreme, no more than 6% in any province express a desire to move to live in Quebec or Nova Scotia, 4% in P.E.I., 3% in Saskatchewan, and 2% in Manitoba, Newfoundland, New Brunswick, or the Territories.

TABLE 9.3 *Desired Province of Residence by Present Province of Residence (In %'s)*

| PROVINCE OF RESIDENCE | PREFERRED PROVINCE | | | | | |
	Own	B.C.	Ontario	Alberta	Others*	Totals
British Columbia	79	—	7	9	5	100
Alberta	63	29	5	—	3	100
Saskatchewan	45	33	5	15	2	100
Manitoba	31	33	12	11	13	100
Ontario	69	18	—	5	8	100
Quebec	64	13	16	4	3	100
New Brunswick	55	19	12	4	10	100
Nova Scotia	67	11	8	5	9	100
Prince Ed. Island**	56	6	22	6	10	100
Newfoundland	48	20	13	7	12	100

*No single other province preference exceeds 5%.
**N=13; while percentages unstable, reported for heuristic value.

If there is a crisis of provincial loyalty and affection, it is within the borders of Manitoba and Saskatchewan. Less than half of the teenagers living in those two prairie provinces want to stay. Saskatchewan is attractive as a permanent place to live for only 45%. Manitoba ranks the lowest in the country at 31%. The harsh reality is that more teenagers in Manitoba would prefer to live in British Columbia (33%) than in their home province!

Some National and Institutional Expectations

We also asked teenagers to assess the future influence of select countries and institutions. Specifically, we asked: "Do you think that by the end of this century, the following will *gain* more influence, *lose* some influence, or remain about the same?" If teenage impressions become actual social trends, there will be some clear winners and losers.

The Winners.   Young people are highly impressed with *science*. Some 85% think science will become even more influential in the future (see table 9.4). Science has been offered to today's teenagers as the great problem solver, the saviour of society. They have been recipients of the benefits of scientific research and technological advances. They live in a day in which space launchings are commonplace. They share first-hand in the computer's take-over of modern life. They feel comfortable in the high-tech age. The only question in most minds is not the nature of science's ongoing impact but rather the nature of its next contribution.

Teenagers also expect that many feminist goals will be implemented by the year 2000. Three-quarters project that *women* will become more influential in the affairs of society. As we have noted, however, teenage theory appears to be preceding their practice. Although they may be as conversant as politicians with the lingo of the "equality of the sexes", "the right of reproductive choice", and "equal pay for equal value", young people are still thinking and acting traditionally.

As a country, *Canada* also stands in the winners' circle. Half of the nation's teenagers anticipate that this country will carry increasing weight in the international community. Here again, young people give further evidence of being positive about their "home and native land".

When it comes to the superpowers, adolescents think Russia and the United States will also gain in influence. The fact that they give the edge to the U.S. (52%) while acknowledging the power of the USSR (42%) may be a blend of realism and wishful thinking.

The Losers.   Compared with their present status in society, *the traditional family, traditional morality*, and *religion* are all seen as losing significant amounts of influence in the future. Such impressions are in keeping with the findings in Chapters Six and Seven concerning the place of family and religion in the lives of young people. Their

TABLE 9.4   *Select National and Institutional Expectations (In %'s)*

	FUTURE INFLUENCE			
	Gain	Same–Gain	Lose	Totals
Institutions				
Science	84	95	5	100
Religion	19	56	44	100
Traditional family	15	44	56	100
Men	26	77	23	100
Women	74	94	6	100
Traditional morality	17	51	49	100
Countries				
Canada	51	87	13	100
United States	52	81	19	100
Russia	42	76	24	100

views concerning the future of traditional morality are *not* consistent with our intergenerational findings. Here teenagers may be reflecting the position of the media and other institutions in believing that their views and lifestyles depart significantly from previous generations. Perhaps reflecting the relatively recent, accelerated industrialized and social change in Quebec, young people there are more likely than their counterparts elsewhere to see the past — in the form of the traditional family, morality, and religion — as being swept away.

The other downward shift in influence envisioned by Canadian young people pertains to gender relations. Corresponding to the perception of 3 in 4 teenagers that women will assert more influence, 1 in 4 anticipate that men will experience a decrease in influence during the next fifteen years.

Assessment

Teenagers give evidence of believing in the Canadian Dream. They believe that individuals have the opportunity through hard work and education to be successful. They believe that, regardless of their own family experiences, marriage and children are major means to the happiness and love they have come to value. Most believe that their lives are best lived in Canada.

In sum, our institutions have come through with flying colours. Young people value the things society indicates they should and are pursuing the things they should. Now the onus is on society to deliver on the promises made by its institutions. It remains to be seen whether or not society can make good on them, particularly in providing the opportunity for the jobs promised to teenagers since pre-school days.

Sociologist Robert Merton pointed out some 50 years ago that stable societies do more than just publicize success goals and thereby inspire dreams.[6] They also provide legitimate means by which their members can achieve those goals. If such means are not available, one possibility is that people will scale down their dreams, lower their expectations, and thereby ensure ongoing social stability. That is clearly one option many have felt obliged to choose. Merton points out, however, that other options for those who retain the dreams and are therefore frustrated by inaccessible means include crime, alcoholism and drug addiction, mental illness, dropping out, and the ultimate "drop-out", suicide. For others who decided to "fight the system", Merton envisions rebellion and even revolution.

This famous typology succinctly lays out the possibilities for a Canadian society that promises much but is in increasing danger of delivering little. For many, where there is hope, there is life. Hope makes the present more enjoyable for some, and at least tolerable for others. It is critically important that we as a society not default on the promised opportunities that have given birth to those hopes and dreams. A Toronto male in grade twelve precisely sums up our sentiments:

> Hopefully teenagers will not stop dreaming and hoping for a better future because if they do there will be even more problems because there won't be anything left to grow up to.

The apparent calmness and contentment of Canadian young people should not be taken by adults to mean that they will remain positive and subdued if it becomes overwhelmingly apparent to them that their society has failed them. The poetry of Journey serves as a warning: in walking through desert sand, there is need for caution as we tread, for "Underfoot are the visions lost,/ Sleeping not yet dead."[7]

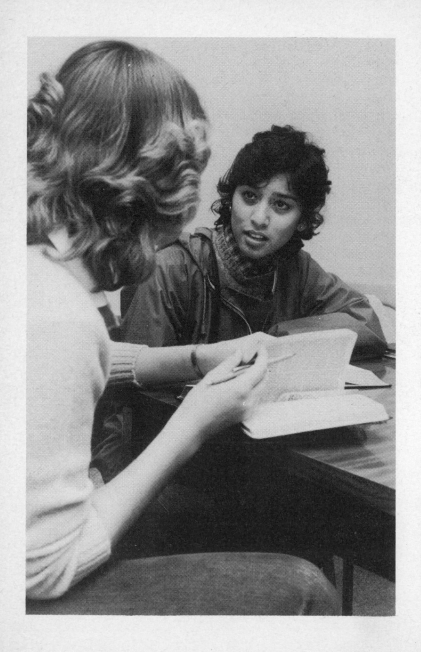

10

RESPONDING TO EMERGENCE

Towards a Resolution of the Problem

Perhaps there would be less problems with the relationship between teenagers and adults if they were encouraged to grow to understand each other and to work and play together.
— a seventeen-year-old female from Vancouver

Past and Present

This is Canada's emerging generation. It is coming of age at a period in history of unequalled scientific and technological progress, a period Orwell and Huxley envisioned would be characterized by revolutionary changes in values, relationships, and family structure.

Canadian young people sense the uniqueness of the times. From Brampton, Ontario, comes this comment from a female who is in grade ten:

> My generation has to face threats and problems that no other generation has had to face before.

A rural Quebec sixteen-year-old makes the observation:

> It's tough growing up in the world. I'm sure it was for you too, only it's getting worse.

At the same time, teenagers feel that generally they are coping fairly well. A Vancouver grade ten female states:

> I think teenagers today are much more adaptable than teenagers 20 years ago. I guess it is because we grew up with the technology.

But however unique this time in history may be, our study has nevertheless revealed not a revolution but, rather, dramatic continuity between past and present. Traditional values regarding friendship, love, and freedom, along with honesty, hard work, and consideration, continue to be of paramount importance in this high-tech age. Relationships remain the primary source of happiness. The foremost source of concern continues to be the immediate future. Sexual attitudes and practices differ little from the generation of the 1950s and 1960s. Belief in the supranatural and religious affiliation are still clearly alive. Respect for other Canadians and their rights exceeds that of previous genera-ations. Social issues, while changing in content with changing times, nevertheless still pertain primarily to "staying alive" and "living well". Dreams, plans, and expectations continue to focus on economic stability and marriage and family.

But before we adults smile, sigh with relief, and drink a toast to the future, we would do well to ponder the implications of the survey's findings.

Grading Our Progress

A recent experience around a banquet table with several other adults was a revelation. Before we could get to the appetizer, a mother with young children started complaining about her teenage babysitter. As she talked her dismay edged into anger. Money was at the centre of the problem. Several weeks prior to the banquet night, the mother, who was in her mid-thirties, had arranged for her regular sitter to care for her children. Just a few days before the banquet, however, her babysitter called to say her regular rates had increased — in fact, they had doubled. The young mother expressed her appreciation for the warning and said she would find another sitter.

Several phone calls later she concluded that the teenagers had banded together at school and formed a babysitters' union. Everyone's rate was the same. By this point in her story, the woman was livid. She proceeded with a standard adult lamentation, "What has become of this younger generation?"

She could just as well have been proud of the teenagers for doing so well what adults do: taking care of number one, demanding rights, politicizing every area of life. In this minor case, as in so many others, teenagers are showing they are learning the adult rules of life, taking their cues from those who have preceded them.

If we wish to evaluate ourselves on the basis of our success at socialization, we probably deserve an "A". Adolescents are close to being miniature models of present-day adults. Teenagers have learned just about everything well. Parents, teachers, government leaders, clergy, and other adults can be proud of their achievement.

If, on the other hand, we add the criterion of encouraging the development of that imagination we saw in our children's early stories and drawings, games and songs, we may have to be dropped to an overall "B". There is something unnerving about being introduced to our clone. And there is disturbingly little difference between us and the coming generation. We may pay a heavy price for cultivating imitation rather than imagination, conformity rather than innovation.

If we also add the criterion of facilitating emergence, sensitively allowing teenagers necessary room to grow, the grade may dip to a low "C". The study findings have consistently suggested that many young people are being "kept in their place" by parents, teachers, and other adults.

Such teenagers will get over being stymied but will pay an ongoing mental, emotional, and social price.

What about our grade for personal integrity? This would be evidenced by our making the ethical and moral demands of ourselves that we have demanded of teens. Further, it would be shown by our ensuring that the opportunities we say exist do, in fact, exist. Adding this criterion, we are probably going to have to settle for an overall grade of "D".

With the findings of this study now firmly in hand, it is time to look more closely at the problem of teenage emergence. In particular, we will focus on teen–parent co-operation, or lack of co-operation, in the process of moving through the stormy waters that often lie between child-hood and adulthood. The picture at first is bleak, showing parental and institutional suppression of emergence. Things turn brighter, however, as we consider how adults and teenagers can work together to take the sting out of adolescence.

The Suppression of Teenage Emergence

The Parent Problem

We are not allowed to criticize our parents. "Right or wrong," says the cultural folklore, "they are still our parents." We are expected to honour them when we are children and respect them in adulthood. If they are deceased, they are usually beyond the pale of criticism.

Yet one of the most common casualties of parental reverence has been the teenager. Not uncommonly teenagers find themselves with parents who are either *unable* or *unwilling* to cope positively with their emergence. However, armed with the adult version of the teenage experience, described at the outset of Chapter One, parents typically give themselves an exemption from blame when conflict arises. The fault is said to lie with the teenager. After all, it is not parents who have changed.

Many adults tend to look at teenagers in keeping with Mark Twain's maxim: "When I was sixteen, I thought my father was a damn fool. When I became twenty-one I was amazed to find how much he had learned in five years." Twain's famous statement is a clever compliment to adults but it is also a subtle put-down of teenagers. It implies that in those turbulent teenage years, adults are wise and adolescents are fools. Parents are elevated as superior human beings while young people are projected as an inferior species.

If adults relate to teenagers with the assumption that they are just passing through a stage that needs to be endured, they will be inclined to treat young people as sub-humans. If they harbour negative biases towards teenagers, their ability to understand and affirm them will be minimized. If adults think they are always the stable reference point in their relationships with adolescents, their superhuman posture will preclude healthful interaction.

So it is that parents commonly frustrate their sons and daughters through their insensitivity and unco-operativeness towards emergence. Yet this action is seldom if ever noticed or condemned by society.

What is particularly intriguing is the way in which teenagers, once they finally become adults, typically become equally blind to their parents' suppression of their own emergence. Ironically, as we grow older we adopt the adult version of the teenage years, despite what we have experienced. It is not unlike the process whereby the poor who become rich forget what it was like to be poor. When we assume adult roles, we feel like adults and we think like adults, complete with the adult myth about teenagers. We consequently tend to *reinterpret* our teenage experience through that framework. We frequently find ourselves taking the blame for how we related to our parents (e.g., "I was really a rotten kid"). In doing so, we tend to remember what was good about them and minimize what was bad. In the process, we absolve them of any responsibility. More seriously, we proceed to use the same interpretation on our own teenagers. The oppressed become the oppressors. The result is that the adult resistance to emergence is passed down from generation to generation, and accorded the status of a virtue.

Obviously there are parents who respond in good faith to teenage emergence but who are simply bewildered by it all. They are not unlike one of the authors' dogs who recently brought her first pup into the world. Ignoring instinctual dogma, she deserted her noisy new arrival and fled to the most remote corner of the house. Unfortunately, precisely at the time when adolescents need them most, parents are often having their own physical, emotional, and career crises.[1] As one writer puts it, "Adolescence arrives at a rather unhandy time ... when middle-aged parents are asking: Who am I, what have I accomplished, where am I now, and what does the future hold for me?"[2]

Beyond innocent bewilderment are a number of personal attributes that can contribute to literally "smothering" emerging teenagers. We would briefly suggest four.

Excessive Control.   A major criterion of responsible parental care of teenagers is control. We socially sanction the "disciplining" of children, which the common dictionary defines in terms of training. The applause for discipline shows no signs of diminishing. A 1980 Gallup Poll revealed that 80% of adults felt "discipline in most homes" is not strict enough; only 1% felt it is too strict. These figures represent little change over time. In 1955, comparable results were 75% and 2% respectively.[3]

However, disciplining, if not motivated by love, can become a means of insensitive control. Parental discipline, in its severe forms, has had less than an impressive track record. The origin of rigid discipline, suggests sociologist

Gerald Leslie, lies in pre-modern times, when "parents were supposed to be strict disciplinarians whose duty it was to break the will of the child" and render him or her submissive.[4] The potential for the abuse of discipline is apparent.

Beyond its "institutional assignment", control is a trait that is highly valued in our society. It is therefore something that can be sorely abused by adults in institutional settings. For example, a father or a mother who has little social power is nevertheless in a position to exercise almost total control over a child. When such control is challenged by the emerging child, one typical response is punishment. A young woman told us that her first severe beating by her father took place when she was *two* years old; it was accompanied by his vow that he "would break her spirit". Here an individual tragedy is bizarrely made possible by a "sacred" and private institution, in the name of a societal virtue.

The threat to adult control obviously becomes greatly magnified when young people reach their teenage years. One youth expert comments, "Adolescents have to fight for freedom, and sometimes the ensuing battle of wills is heated."[5] Psychologist E.J. Anthony writes, "With every artifice at their command, certain parents will attempt to close the doors and raise the drawbridges and dig deep moats to keep their burgeoning offspring in, for they cannot bring themselves to realize that the loss entailed is almost as inevitable as death and almost as irreversible."[6] Problems and conflict with parents, teachers, and other authority figures are inevitable if these adults insist on "keeping teenagers in their place" — that is, as subordinate and inferior human beings. Parents who punish their adolescents excessively "to make a point", or teachers who try to humiliate them "to set an example" are only rejecting productivity, stymying emergence, and inviting resentment. Research indicates that the usual effect of excessive control is to produce a combination of dependency and rebellion. Meeker adolescents are intimidated; stronger ones are rebellious.[7]

Tragedies sometimes occur when parents are guilty of over-protection and excessive control. When teenagers are denied pathways to emergence, they often over-react. The drive for independence is powerful. When it is blocked, irrational forces can take over. In extreme cases, young women denied dating privileges assert their independence by getting pregnant. Teenagers who live in over-zealous religious homes announce they "no longer believe in God" and refuse to go to church. Young people whose parents rule family life like military generals are caught for shoplifting. Pushed too hard to make the honour roll, adolescents with high IQs bring home report cards with failing grades.

In less extreme cases, teens grow up with unpleasant memories of the bickering that went on in their homes during the teenage years. Love and respect between parents and children as the latter leave and start their own families proves difficult to maintain, if the effort is made at all.

Clearly, control must gradually be yielded in accordance with the ability of emerging teenagers to assume the same level of responsibility as other "full-fledged people". Control for control's sake is a pointless sham.

Vicarious Dreams.   It is widely recognized that the hopes and plans of teenagers are frequently inspired by their parents and other adults. The typical scenario stresses how a mother or a father, a teacher or a coach "gave me a dream, and helped me to achieve it".

In the midst of such heart-warming testimonials, it is easy to overlook a related pattern that is probably far more common to counsellors and psychiatrists, as well as to most of the rest of us. That scenario reveals how mothers and fathers not only provided their offspring with dreams, but also provided them with tremendous pressure to ensure that parental dreams for their children were realized. Social, educational, and occupational goals are laid out for a child. Approval or disapproval depends on the child's willingness to adopt such a parental game-plan. It stands in sharp contrast to the sensitive exploration of the child's interests and abilities, with a respect for individuality.

Parents often come precariously close to trying to "create children in their own images", with these images taking both real and idealized forms. The doctor may expect the same level of education for his son; the clerk may expect a graduate degree for her daughter. Familiar phrases such as, "We want you to amount to something," "I don't want you to go through what I did," "You'd make your father so happy," and "We had such great hopes for you," tell the story of vicarious dreams.

Using sports as an example, Elkind goes so far as to say that he thinks that there may be a strong tie between a father's job dissatisfaction and a disproportionate concern with an offspring's success: "Children thus become the symbols or carriers of their parents' frustrated competitiveness in the work place. The parents can take pride in the child's success or blame the coach for his or her failure. In any case, the parent soon vicariously invests more of a commitment in the child's athletic life than in his or her own work life."[8]

Envy. The "flipside" of vicarious dreaming is the tendency for parents and other adults to be *jealous* of young people. A father, at a time when he himself knows his goals are beyond his grasp, may watch with pain as his son embarks on an exciting career. A mother may realize that her daughter exceeds her own attractiveness and social agility. One such mother admitted to a researcher, "I find myself competitive and jealous of my teenage daughter. She grows more luscious, and I feel like I am drying up."[9] Similarly, a teacher may find that a student exeeds his own creativity. A minister perhaps notes that the sheer freedom of young people greatly contrasts with his expectation-ridden existence. Each in his or her own way may often be murmuring, "Oh, to be young again." As they look at teenagers, adults can and often do envy their looks, their abilities, their energy, their freedom, their opportunities, their accomplishments and, of course, their youth. Psychologist Edward Dreyfus sums up parental envy as follows:

> Parents are afraid and envious; they would like to be as free as youth seems to be . . . They would like to quit a dull job, get out of a boring marriage, change their lives, but are afraid to lose the security. When they see young people violating all of the taboos they themselves have been wanting to violate, they become defensive and angry, stating in effect, if I cannot have it, neither will you — why should you do something I cannot — or would not dare. I suspect that underneath the most irate adult there is considerable envy.[10]

Sometimes adults readily acknowledge such envy, thereby largely defusing its destructive influence. Commonly, however, the envy goes unrecognized or denied. In these instances, teenagers pay a price. Envy contaminates interaction. Much of the energy of the adult is given to trying to establish false superiority. In the process, the worth of the teenager is falsely devalued. Motives for control, when exercised, subsequently become polluted.

In other words, Cinderella is not the only attractive young person who has had her looks downplayed by her mother, and princes have also been known to be devalued by envious kings. Mozart to his death had his talents downplayed by his teacher. Many a talented young person has had abilities treated as disabilities and been told to mask the marvellous and master the mundane.

Envied characteristics bring forth an array of curious responses. Pluses are treated as minuses: "You've got to have more than good looks." School tasks become more important than creative non-conformity: "Sure, it's good, but it's not what I asked for." And when all else fails, one can always pull rank: "It's not bad. In time, with work, who knows . . . ?" These responses are particularly dangerous when coming from adults with power over young people. Albert Einstein, no less, offers this powerful reminder: "Great spirits have always encountered violent opposition from mediocre minds."

Perennial Parenthood. For many fathers and mothers, the power and authority inherent in the parental role are viewed by them as never-ending. They are permanent qualities given to them, almost as a gift "from the gods".

The practical result is that they see themselves as being in unchallenged control of their sons and daghters when they are small children, when they are teenagers, and when they are adults. Such a posture is obviously incompatible with the fact of emergence. Parents who see "their reign" as infinite insist on the retention of a superior adult status to their emerging teenagers. In addition, they frequently see themselves — by self-ascription rather than by actual achievement — as having a superior grasp of life.

The result? Their offspring go through successive stages of obeying them as children, resisting them as teenagers, and ignoring them as adults. When one is a child, subordination seems appropriate. When one is an adolescent, it is stifling. When one is an adult, it is unacceptable.

The major problem here is that these kinds of parents assume "a fixed status" that is simply incongruent with the changing status of their sons and daughters. They are exemplified by the father who still treats his son as a little boy, by the mother who still tells her daughter how to keep the house, and by the in-law who offers unsolicited advice. One study of more than 5,000 Americans married from periods ranging from a few weeks to more than 40 years found that 75% had one or more in-law problems.[11] Life with such parents is not always easy; not surprisingly, the perennial parenthood phenomenon lies behind the tendency of most North Americans — 90% in the U.S. — to feel that parents should not live with their adult children.[12]

While we tend to be fatalistic ("That's just the way Mom is") or make light of such realities (e.g., through mother-in-law jokes), it is time we were honest. When children fail to develop properly, we say that they're experiencing "arrested development". We "medicalize" their "differentness" and see it as a problem. Why, then, do we continue to take lightly the fact that parents very commonly "fail to develop" with their children, instead imposing outdated behaviour that is no longer appropriate? In the case of a six-year-old who wants to act like a baby, we show concern. In the case of a sixty-year-old who wants to act like a father with small children, we show tolerance. But there is nothing healthy, edifying, or humorous about a fifty-year-old mother telling her daughter how to arrange her house and raise her children. The same is true of mothers or fathers who insist on treating their children as infants or their teenagers as little children.

In the face of reverence shown parents, it seems almost sacrilegious to say it, but it needs to be said: such parents suffer from arrested development. Put less politely, they are "relationally handicapped".

Sadly, in reality, perennial parents are shown no favours. They ultimately pay for their inability to develop. Not being able to let their offspring emerge as full and equal human beings, not being able to learn from them, not ceasing to relinquish control, they are eventually treated as largely irrelevant. They are subsidized by our silence and pacified by our politeness. They are not taken seriously. The irony is that, because these fathers and mothers do not treat their children as complete people, they themselves end up suffering the same fate.

The Institutional Problem

Other major institutions besides the family — the school, the media, the workplace, the church or synagogue — also both contribute to teenage emergence as well as inhibit it.

What any of us become at any point in our lifelong experience of emergence is hardly left up to chance. Through its institutions, societies such as ours instil appropriate behaviour and attitudes. This "socialization" process through which we learn how to become "participant members of society" spans our lifetimes.

Since the goal of socialization is to impart the cultural resources that will enable new members "to play the societal game", a heavy emphasis is placed on mastering existing material. That body of information includes everything from the alphabet through how to dress and eat to what to value, believe, and practise. Such learning understandably maximizes memorizing and the unreflective compilation of cultural information.

A heavy emphasis is also placed on learning to follow the proper rules or norms. We say what we are supposed to say. We do the things expected of us. We don't make waves. To the extent that individuals stick to their role prescriptions, they literally come to be designated as "good". Norm conformity is what we usually have in mind when we label an individual as a "good" boy or a "good" girl, a "good" student or a "good" employee, a "good" parent or a "good" citizen, and, in eulogy form, a "good" man or a "good" woman. They follow the rules. People described thus are not obnoxious or eccentric, weird or mentally ill, obscene or immoral, delinquent or criminal, rebellious or revolutionary. Further, a "good" parent is one who has "good" children. Conversely, having a "bad" teenager, for example, calls into question both the character and the competence of a mother or father.

Institutions, however, can seriously suppress emergence in at least two major ways.

Excessive Normality.   While socialization is essential to group life, the importance placed on learning "the right" ideas and "the right" behaviour can clearly go beyond simply teaching human birds how to fly. If emphasized at the expense of individual reflection and the exploration of individual creativity, the process can be oppressive. Emerging young people who want to question life can find the process stifling. Socialization can become like that medieval box used to make children grow into distorted shapes.

Mitchell makes the important point that staying out of trouble at school, not breaking the law, and avoiding family conflict may be indicative of a young person's being "well-adjusted". However, he says, avoiding trouble "is not the mark of a healthy adolescent if it is achieved at the expense of sapping initiative, stifling creativity, dampening youthful spontaneity, or fostering acquiescence as a lifestyle".[13] When in an environment out of keeping with one's needs, he suggests, the *healthy* young person will resist, renounce, and rebel.

If not committed to a respect for individuality and critical reflection, in addition to the mastery of existing material, our major institutions will function as socialization assembly lines. In the words of one writer, schools in particular will simply see young people as "empty bottles on an assembly line of grades — each grade [filling] the bottle up a little more, the bottle representing the child's memory".[14] Teenagers and others will hold "the right ideas" and follow "the right" rules, yet largely be void of individuality.

Tragically, the creed of conformity has the possibility of designating difference as a liability, regardless of its relationship, positive or negative, to the life of a society. Creative people — artists, writers, scientists, leaders — are typically different from the norm. It is no accident that we speak of "the mad scientist", the "eccentric inventor", or "the absent-minded professor". Michelangelo, Martin Luther, Albert Einstein, Thomas Edison, Winston Churchill, and our own Mackenzie King were all regarded as "different". Note the following two profiles:

> Boy not a good all-around student . . . has no friends . . .
> teachers find him a problem . . . spoke late . . . father

ashamed of son's lack of athletic ability ... poor adjustment to school. ... Parents regard him as "different."

Boy, aged six, head large at birth ... mother does not
agree with relatives and neighbors that child is probably abnormal. Child sent to school, diagnosed as mentally ill by teacher. Mother is angry. Withdraws child
from school, says she will teach him herself.[15]

The students described? The first, Albert Einstein, the
second, Thomas Edison.

Society has to be flexible enough to give creatively different people room to breathe. Otherwise the emerging
inventor and visionary, the artist and national leader, will
all be thrown out with the classroom garbage.

Misuse of Power. Further, because of their power and
freedom, institutions are in a position to seriously suppress the emergence of teenagers and others. Along with
parents, our teachers, lawyers, the police, judges, business
executives, doctors, politicians, and media representatives
tend to enjoy a rather exalted status. It does not take a
social scientist to recognize that the relationships of parent–
child, teacher–student, policeman–citizen, lawyer–client,
priest–parishioner, and doctor–patient do not involve equal
status. The institutional "representative" is clearly in charge,
while the other is the subordinate.

Institutions have a great amount of freedom. Individuals of all ages who of necessity are exposed to them are
placed in highly vulnerable positions against which society
provides few safeguards. For example, only when it becomes
known that a parent or a teacher has acted in an extremely
unacceptable manner does society even consider inter-
vening to protect individuals being "serviced" by families
and schools. The same can be said of the surveillance of
policing practices, religious activities, court decisions, or
hospital and nursing home care.

To the extent that teenagers and others have difficulty
when interacting with institutions, the problems are typi-

cally seen as resting with the person, and not with the institution. This is particularly a problem when the individual involved is under age. A child who is seen to "disobey" her parent is viewed as "a bad girl", regardless of the unreasonableness of the demand placed upon her. A schoolboy who is in conflict with a teacher is typically labelled, significantly, as *"insubordinate"*, despite the fact that his reaction may have been unnecessarily provoked by the teacher. A teenager with long hair driving an older model car is seen as deserving the speeding ticket, even though he probably was "selectively stopped" in the first place.

Like parents, these institutions and their adult representatives are frequently not sensitive to the reality of emergence. Rather, they are so preoccupied with "keeping people in their place" — with control as an end in itself — that they often suffocate teenagers and others, psychologically and emotionally. Understandably, they are commonly viewed by teenagers with antagonism.

Thus it is that a grade one teacher, who poorly disguises her animosity towards a six-year-old, is allowed to tell a beleaguered parent, "I feel like I have to compete with your son for the leadership of the class." Her control threatened by a first-grader with exceptional skills, she responds not with an effort to channel or co-opt his abilities, but with hostility and detentions. This sort of behaviour led an education editor of *Saturday Review* to say, "Behind prisons and the military, the schools are the third most authoritarian institutions in America."[16] Inflexible schools, churches, and other institutions are on a collision course with emerging young people.

The Price Paid for the Problem

The suppression of teenage emergence by parents and institutions is tragic not simply because it creates conflict. That conflict is merely symptomatic of the more serious problem. A human life is trying to emerge. But it is being denied the room to grow by the adults who have been given charge over it. The pain will eventually disappear. The conflict will pass. The struggle will cease. And the life will emerge. Depending on the space it was given, that life will sometimes be normal. Other times, however, it will be distorted and deformed. One psychologist puts it succinctly: "Few young people survive youth without emotional and psychic damage."[17]

Towards Co-operative Emergence

A positive response to the problems surrounding teenage emergence does not lie in taking either a "pro-adult" or "pro-teenager" position. Books written from the viewpoint of adults, such as *Toughlove,* can readily be countered by works such as *The Oppression of Youth,* which comes from the teenage corner of the ring. While such writings can help sensitize us to the problems of both combatants and while undoubtedly both apply to extreme teenage and adult cases, they have an adversarial, single-actor emphasis that, we feel, is neither particularly accurate nor constructive.

In the early 1970s, an American educational expert, Robert Barr, wrote: "Many of our youth are deeply troubled, and they believe that they have few allies providing them support. Our exisitng institutions — the family, the school, the church, and the courts — have often seemed to deepen their alienation rather than to alleviate the problems."[18] There is no need for such erosion to take place.

If we value optimum living within the family, within institutions, and within our society as a whole, then it is hoped we will be receptive to the consideration of modifications that can make life happier for all of us. Accordingly, we believe that positive responses to problems surrounding teenage emergence need to be made and can be made on the part of parents, institutions, and young people themselves.

The Response of Adults

If adults are to play a positive role in facilitating teenage emergence, they must start by being clearly aware of the reality of emergence. Parents, teachers, youth leaders, coaches, ministers, friends, and others need to grasp explicitly the idea that an adult is literally being born. That person needs understanding, encouragement, and help. Above all, he or she needs room to grow.

But this is not to say that child–adult hybrids simply need to have the way cleared in order to develop naturally and autonomously. We are not for a moment advocating some kind of laissez-faire approach. Obviously children require the direction and the help of adults if they are to become human in any meaningful social and moral sense.

However, the delicate balance lies in adults' providing sufficient direction while at the same time knowing when it can be relinquished. This, of course, means there has to be a willingness on the part of adults to "let go".

Psychologist Elkind describes this process with clarity. In early childhood, children want to take liberties for which they may not be ready. A child may want to lift a glass, and the parent must be able to assess accurately the child's competence. As long as children understand that they will have more chances later, he says, withholding freedoms after some exploratory failures can help them come to grips with their own limits. As children grow, parents and other adults need to allow them to take progressive responsibility for their behaviour.[19]

Ideally, adults will sensitively monitor the young person's level of intellectual, social, and emotional development in order to provide the appropriate freedom and opportunity for responsibility. When this is not done, continues Elkind, significant interpersonal damage can occur. He concludes that, in the case of the family, "when there is a reasonably close match between parental expectations and child performance and between child expectations and parental performance, there is relatively little stress in family interactions."[20]

In short, if parents and other adults can maintain that balance between providing direction and relinquishing it, "storm and stress" is not inevitable. The accuracy of our observation that such a balance is needed can be tested using the data of our own biographies. With few exceptions, if our parents literally "allowed us to grow up", relinquishing ground as we became able to assume it, we had a fairly tranquil adolescence. If one parent could let us grow up and the other could not, we have little difficulty isolating the parent with whom we were able to feel more comfortable. If neither one gave us room to become an adult, we undoubtedly felt alienated from both of them. Accordingly, some of us enjoyed home life during those years. Others ran away or moved away early.

The same pattern characterized our relations with other adults. Invariably the teacher, leader, or coach we liked best was the person who treated us as "a full person" — who did not make us feel as if we had to suppress part of ourselves when in their company. We felt accepted. Conversely, memories of adults we did not like are commonly associated with people who dominated us, who did not take an interest in us, who did not make us feel like whole people.

What we are emphasizing, then, is the importance for adults of becoming sensitized to the reality of teenage emergence and, further, of responding positively to it both by providing resources and by withdrawing them as they no longer are required.

The Response of Institutions

Obviously the institutional and adult responses are only analytically distinct, since adults control major institutions. Nevertheless, there are some features unique to specific institutions that need to be considered when reflecting on how teenage emergence might be more happily accomplished.

The Family.   There are a number of basic ways in which parents deal with their adolescents.[21] One method is to be autocratic, making all decisions by themselves. This usually produces a combination of rebellion on the one hand and dependency on the other. A second route is the permissive one, whereby parents allow the adolescent more influence than themselves in making decisions. Research suggests that such teenagers have a number of subsequent problems in relating to others, often being domineering, self-centred, and impatient, as well as indecisive and insecure. A third possibility is a democratic style. Here decisions are made jointly by parents and teenagers. This approach is seen as having the most positive effect on adolescents. Parents continue to provide guidance, yet encourage young people to show responsibility, initiative, and autonomy. In the words of F. Philip Rice, "As a result the home atmosphere is likely to be one of respect, appreciation, warmth, and acceptance."[22] Finally, in homes where parental styles are erratic and inconsistent, confusion predictably results.

Given the reality of emergence, its complexity and difficulty, it is hardly surprising that teenagers want a blend of security and autonomy from their parents. Young people want to be given the opportunity to make choices, to exert their own independence, to negotiate with adults and assume responsibility. But few want complete freedom, for now.

Rice maintains that a compilation of extensive research findings indicate that adolescents want and need parents who:

"Are interested in us and available to help us when needed."

"Listen to us and try to understand us."

"Talk with us, not at us."

"Love and accept us as we are, faults and all."

"Trust us and expect the best of us."

"Discipline us fairly."

". . . admit when they have made a mistake."[23]

The School. Ernest Boyer refers to the school as "the one institution where it is all right to be young".[24] Professor Elkind, in contrast, charges that the "scandal of our schools is their failure to provide a protected place for teenagers to struggle with the difficult task of growing up . . . a protected place in which they can get on with the task of building an identity".[25] Volumes have been written and continue to be written on the school and its shortcomings, and on the steps necessary to remedy its problems. Few institutions are more frequently assailed.

It is not our purpose to attempt a major critique of the schools. We would, however, reiterate how important it is for school personnel, notably teachers, to comprehend the nature of emergence and attempt to be responsive to it. Since, as Mitchell puts it, the school "is the dominant fact of youth existence",[26] the role of school personnel is critical to the successful and enjoyable movement of young people into adulthood.

This means treating students as persons who matter, attempting to empathize with their struggles and, to the extent that it is humanly possible, responding to them as individuals. Concern for material mastery and order should not be allowed to become obsessive so that it obliterates imagination and reflection, along with creative difference. This is what makes teaching, in the words of educator Baughman, "a dangerous profession". "The philosophies, strategies, and objectives" — and, we would add, interpersonal relations — "may either stunt or nourish emotions and intellect."[27]

So far as curriculum is concerned, being responsive to emergence means continuing the never-ending search for ways of making the time spent in school a time that is in tune with the interests and the needs of young people, as well as "the world out there". As educators know well, if not seen as a place for meaningful learning opportunities, the school is destined to have primarily a custodial function for young people, complete with complaints that school is boring and irrelevant.

The Church.   In addition to taking seriously the importance of recognizing the reality of emergence, religious organizations that wish to be effective in retaining teenagers and appealing to those who are unchurched seem to face three major hurdles. The first is *how to be authoritative without being authoritarian*, thereby offering direction without negating the freedom that is integral to emergence. A central task of religious groups is not just to indoctrinate but also to help young people think through religious ideas in order to develop a faith that has meaning for them.[28] One Catholic scholar, for example, suggests that such a position is consistent with Vatican II's emphasis on faith being an open and free response to God.[29]

The second hurdle involves *finding ways to provide support without creating a subculture* — an environment that can be responsive to the desire for friendship and caring without alienating teenagers from the youth milieu of which they are a part.

The third is *how to focus on transcendence without trivializing life*, relating simultaneously to the 50% who want religion to deal with spiritual matters and to the other 50%, who expect religion to address everyday concerns. The task that these three issues present is formidable but, in our opinion, not insurmountable.

Historically, the Christian church has travelled on the main thoroughfares in Canadian society. In the past 25 years, however, the church has been pushed aside by other traffic and been forced to travel on secondary highways. The inclination of adults who have chosen to live without the church is to impose their choices on the next generation, an inclination clearly not in the interests of co-operative emergence. Elkind offers good counsel and a word of caution: "Religion speaks to a deep and abiding need in all of us, or it could not have survived. Religion provides a perspective beyond ourselves and our world that helps us to manage the existential problem of realizing our significance and place in the universe. If we do not have a religious faith ourselves, we should not deny it or denigrate it to our offspring."

Government. Young people are sending two clear messages to the governments of this country. First, they want an opportunity for more input into society. They feel they have a contribution to make, and want the chance to make it. Second, they want jobs. Rightly or wrongly, they are going to expect the leaders of the country, namely governments, to come through. The failure for such expectations to be realized will result in disenchantment of enormous proportions.

The University of Alberta's John Mitchell is among the most vocal among those decrying "the adolescent predicament" of having much to provide but few avenues for meaningful contribution. He writes that we "are wasting the energy, ambition, and talent of our youth" and that "most youth who idle away their hours are themselves seeking something important to do."[31]

He would like to see the energy and ability of youth integrated with the needs of society, "such that both parties benefit". Mitchell proposes a number of ways in which students, through their schools, might contribute to their communities and thereby not only "learn about their society" but also address their personal needs for "positive contribution and worthwhile work".[32]

Governments at various levels have been forced to respond to the present and impending employment crises involving young people. But as noted earlier, the problems are far from solved. In her November 14, 1984, speech to the House of Commons, Canada's Youth Minister, Andrée Champagne, acknowledged that the nation's young people "will not understand any delay. They are demanding action, and rightly so." She indicated that forthcoming programs will be aimed at solving youth unemployment, discarding short-term solutions in favour of attacking "the roots of the problem facing us and not just its effects".

Champagne also indicated that she wanted to hear from teenagers: "I want to listen to young people," she said, "to learn more about their problems and their achievements . . ."

She promised that in 1985, the United Nations' International Youth Year, she would introduce a policy and proposals that would "contribute to increasing youth participation in all sectors of our society".[33] The nature and impact of such government promises remain to be seen.

The Response of Teenagers

If emergence into adulthood is to be a positive experience for all concerned, teenagers also have a pivotal role to play in the social process. They, as well as adults, need to develop an awareness of their "hybrid" status and the problems it raises for everyone involved. Teenagers need to be given assistance in comprehending what emergence involves for them and also what it involves for parents and other adults. Presumably, adults should be the ones who at least initiate the exposition of the nature of emergence.

For example, one of the authors made a point of taking his three sons aside, one by one, as they entered their early adolescence years, and explaining the problem he was up against. He conveyed the dilemma that parents face when they are trying to relate to offspring who are "half-child and half-adult". In each instance, those early discussions provided a reference-point for subsequent discussions pertaining to the fine line between control and freedom.

Beyond developing an awareness of the nature of emergence and the problems it raises for adults and teenagers, adolescents should also realize that "parents are people, too." As the authors of *Toughlove* put it, beyond being obsessed with young people and their needs, everyone needs to recognize that adults also need to be loved. "Parents," they write, "have feelings and needs that require attention from their children."[34] Teenagers who want to be taken seriously as people have to reciprocate when dealing with adults.

Further, if emergence is to be successful and positive, adolescents must be prepared to emerge. Some are not. A number of observers have drawn attention to the fact that some young people do not want to grow up. They are like chicks who prefer to stay in the safety of the shell. Such individuals prolong adolescence as a social role, which they retain well into their twenties and even beyond. They remain dependent on their parents; they do not "grow up".

Relatedly, adolescents who are emerging into adulthood have obligations to their family and society. In Mitchell's words, "Adolescence is not a time zone in which the person acquires immunity from social responsibility, nor is it a time when one is exempt from helping others or contributing to the general welfare."[35] The old adage "If you want your freedom, be willing to accept responsibility" applies to teenagers.

We believe that if adults and teenagers can reach such a point where both are aware of the nature of emergence and both are prepared to see it through together, treating each other with the respect due not to parents or teenagers but to human beings, adolescence can be a positive and enjoyable experience.

Elkind warns about the danger of treating life stages as stepping stones to better things. "If we really value human life," he suggests, "we will value each period equally and give unto each stage of life what is appropriate to that stage."[36] The positive aspects of our own adolescent years, we repeat, were no accident. They were invariably tied to encountering people who allowed us to become what we were becoming. The teenage years can be good years if young people and adults, in the interest of enjoyable living, will work towards co-operative emergence.

Such a possibility would be welcomed by many teenagers who are finding adolescence tough. Among them is a fifteen-year-old from a small Manitoba community who comments:

> I would like to say that adults should talk to teenagers more often. I wish I could talk to adults more often, but they never seem to have time. They only have time to catch us doing something wrong.

A grade eleven female from rural Alberta offers a similar view:

> Why don't you send one of your surveys to the parents, because some families don't get along and it's not always the teenagers, it's also the parents. Maybe then some kids could understand their parents more.

The challenge facing Canadian adults can be summed up in the succinct line on a plaque hanging in a school principal's office:

> We give our children roots — and wings.

APPENDIX

The Teen Canada Survey

The national survey entitled "Project Teen Canada" was conducted during the four months of May, June, September, and October of 1984. The survey was carried out from the University of Lethbridge, with Bibby serving as project director and Posterski as associate director.

Sample Size. A sample of 3,600 teenagers was pursued, a figure that, if representatively selected, makes it possible to generalize to the overall adolescent population (2.3 million) with a high level of accuracy (within about three percentage points, either way, 19 times in 20). A sample of that size also increases the accuracy of analyses within the aggregate — such as breakdowns by gender, region, and community size — over that, for example, of a typical Gallup survey with a Canadian national sample size of about 1,100 cases.

The Sampling Frame. In attempting to probe the emerging generation, that segment of young people on the verge of becoming adults, the decision was made to restrict the sample to

Canadians fifteen to nineteen years old. Ideally, a national sample of these teenagers would involve a random selection of all teenagers in this age group in the country. From a methodological point of view, however, such a task is a formidable one. Problems include the establishment of an adequate sampling frame, accessibility, and, for some, parental consent.

Consequently, the sampling frame was limited to teenagers aged fifteen to nineteen in grades ten to twelve across Canada. (This included CEGEPs in Quebec.) These three grades encompass some two-thirds of those in this age group. Moreover, some 65% of the remaining one-third not in high school were there for one year or more. We therefore maintain that to get a reading of secondary students is to get a highly comprehensive snapshot of the emerging generation as it passes through high school.

Sampling Procedures.   In pursuing the sample size goal of 3,600 high-school students, the decision was made to randomly select individual high-school classrooms rather than individual students, because of the significant administrative advantages and minimal negative consequences for a random sample. The design involved choosing one classroom in each school selected. Based on an average class size of perhaps 25 students, this meant that some 150 schools needed to participate (N=3750). On the basis of a projected response rate of about 75%, approximately 200 schools were selected to comprise the sample.

The schools were chosen using multi-stage stratified and cluster sampling procedures. The country was first stratified according to the five major regions, with each region then stratified according to community size (100,000 and over, 99,000 to 10,000, less than 10,000). Each community size category was in turn stratified according to school system (public, separate, private).

Specific communities within each size stratum were then randomly selected, with the number of communities drawn from each province in the Prairie and Atlantic regions based on population. Finally, one school in each of these communities was chosen randomly. The number of schools selected in cities with a population above 100,000 was proportional to their population in their region. The specific grade of the classroom involved was also randomly designated.

TABLE A1 *School Participation in the Survey by Region (Actual Numbers)*

	Required	Pursued	In	Refusals	Non-Res.	Rate
British Columbia	15	20	14	5	1	70%
Prairies	27	43	33	6	4	77%
Ontario	52	64	46	12	6	72%
Quebec	41	49	39	2	8	80%
Atlantic	15	24	20	2	2	83%
Totals	150	200	152	27	21	76%

The Administration of the Survey. Guidance counsellors at each school were contacted, and asked to (i) choose a classroom which they viewed as representative of the requested grade, and (ii) personally administer the questionnaire. They were instructed to stress that participation was voluntary and that anonymity and confidentiality would be honoured. The counsellors were asked to place completed questionnaires in the pre-paid postal envelope provided "in full view of the students", and to seal the envelope in their presence.

The Response. Questionnaires were returned from 152 of the 200 designated classrooms — a return rate of 76% (see Table A1). The remaining 48 schools either declined to participate (27) or did not respond to requests to do so (21).

A total of 3,664 questionnaires were received, with 134 of these discarded because they had been filled out by students younger than fifteen or older than nineteen. The number of useable questionnaires thus totalled 3,530.

Representativeness. As Table A2 shows, the sample in its raw, unweighted form is fairly representative of the Canadian population of fifteen- to nineteen-year-olds. It has, however, been weighted for region and community size on a regional basis (fifteen weight factors). In its final, weighted form, the sample is highly representative of Canadians in this age group. The minor

TABLE A2	Characteristics of the Teenage (15–19)		
	Teen Pop.*	Unwtd. Sample	Weighted Sample
Nationally			
Survey size	3,600	3,530	3,599
Region			
British Columbia	10	9	10
Prairies	18	24	18
Ontario	35	30	35
Quebec	27	23	27
Atlantic	10	14	10
Community Size			
100,000 & over	49	37	50
99,000–10,000	15	16	14
Under 10,000	36	47	36
Gender			
Male	51	48	49
Female	49	52	51
School System			
Public	85	84	85
Separate	10	11	10
Private	5	5	5

variations that do exist seem to reflect methodology rather than differences between the population and the sample. Marital status for thirty-five to fifty-nine-year-old adults is only a crude estimate of the marital status of the parents of teenagers, containing more single people. Population religious affiliation for teenagers has often been given to the census takers by adults. It seems that some adolescents with parents who claim "residual" United Church affiliation (often being inactive yet saying they are United) show a tendency to see themselves as "Nones" rather than United Church when speaking for themselves.

Population and Teen Canada Sample (In %'s)

	Teen Pop.*	Unwtd. Sample	Weighted Sample
Parental Marital Status*			
Married	85	86	86
Divorced	5	8	8
Widowed	3	5	5
Never married	7	1	1
Religion			
Roman Catholic	51	50	51
Protestant	40	36	35
Anglican	9	8	8
Baptist	3	3	3
Lutheran	3	2	2
Pentecostal	2	2	2
Presbyterian	3	2	2
United Church	15	11	10
Other Protestant	5	8	7
Jew	1	1	1
Other	1	2	2
None	7	11	12

Sources: Statistics Canada, 1981 census publications. Regional populations and gender, 92-901, Table 2; community size, 92-901, Table 6; school systems, 81-210, Table 1; marital status 92-901, Table 4; religion, 92-912, Table 3.
**Population data*: marital status of adults ages 35-59.

The sample, then, is both sufficiently large and representative of Canadian teenagers fifteen to nineteen to permit generalizations to the population with a very high level of accuracy. On most items in the questionnaire, the national results should come within about three percentage points of the results of other surveys probing the teenage population, 19 times in 20.

NOTES

Introduction

1. Ishwaran and Chan, 1979:97.
2. Elkind, 1982:xii.
3. Elkind, 1981:135.
4. Elkind, 1981:135.
5. Mitchell, 1975.
6. Barbieri, 1978:505–508.
7. Miller, 1969:introduction.
8. Mitchell, 1975:35.
9. Grabb, 1980.
10. Hobart, 1981.
11. See, for example, McLuhan, 1964; Elkind, 1981:74–75.

Chapter 1

1. Mitchell, 1975:21–22.
2. For an excellent exposition of this point of view, see Peter Berger, 1963:106.
3. Mead, 1950; Benedict, 1950.
4. See, for example, Flake-Hobson, Robinson, and Skeen, 1983:416.
5. Cited in Baughman, 1972:10.

Chapter 2

1. Associated Press release, November 21, 1984.
2. Canadian Institute of Public Opinion, December 1, 1982.
3. Kerr, 1964:168.
4. Rokeach, 1975.
5. Mitchell, 1975:76–77.
6. Elkind, 1981:190.
7. *The Toronto Star*, August 25, 1984: Al.
8. See, for example, Sebald, 1981, vs. Coleman, 1961.
9. "The Logical Song", Almo Music Corp., 1979.
10. Fasick, 1984:147–148.
11. Barr, 1971:13.
12. See, for example, Westhues, 1975.
13. Westhues, 1975:401.
14. Block and Smith, 1968.
15. For examples of such studies, see Rice, 1981:251–252.
16. Rice, 1981:4.
17. Flake-Hobson, Robinson, and Skeen, 1983:445.
18. Baum, 1975:ii.
19. "1984", Mainman, Chryalis, Bewlay, 1973.
20. Clark, 1975:59–60.
21. "It's Hard", Eel Pie Publishing Limited, 1982.
22. Goodman, 1960:x.

Chapter 3

1. Broderick, 1966.
2. "Second to None", Almo Music Corp., 1983.
3. Lambert, Yackley, and Hein, 1971.
4. Toman, 1961.
5. Rice, 1981:377.
6. Elkind, 1981:89.
7. For study examples, see Larson and Kubey, 1983:16.
8. Bibby, 1982.
9. Larson and Kubey, 1983:29.
10. Canadian Press release, September 5, 1984.
11. Canadian Press release, September 17, 1984.
12. Rice, 1981:269.
13. Faulkes, 1984:7.
14. Levine and Stumpf, 1983:430.
15. Barnett, 1984.
16. Levine and Stumpf, 1983:433.
17. See, for example Ramsey, 1967; Grinder, 1973; Rice, 1981.
18. Mackie, 1983a:83.
19. Larson and Kubey, 1983.
20. Larson and Kubey, 1983:25.
21. "On the Loose", Pocket Music, 1981.
22. Elkind, 1981:85.
23. "Music Time", Stygian Songs, 1984.
24. Bibby, 1982.
25. McCormack, 1979:307.
26. American Press release, November 9, 1984.
27. Canadian Press release, September 17, 1984.
28. Ellis, 1983:8.
29. Rice, 1981:267–268.

30. Rice, 1981:268.
31. Rice, 1981:484.
32. Cited in Rice, 1981:482, 484.
33. Rice, 1981:484.
34. Mitchell, 1975:239.
35. Poole, 1984.
36. "The Things That Dreams Are Made Of", Virgin Records Limited, 1981.
37. Davis, 1940.
38. Baughman, 1972:30.
39. Mackie, 1983a:81.
40. Baughman, 1972:27.
41. Brown, 1980:121.

Chapter 4

1. Havighurst, 1972.
2. Flake Hobson, Robinson, and Skeen, 1983:417.
3. See, for example, Shainess, 1961; Pomeroy, 1968.
4. Cited in Rice, 1981:89.
5. Cited in Rice, 1981:89.
6. Agnew, 1984:285–286.
7. See Sontag, 1971.
8. Flake-Hobson, Robinson, and Skeen, 1983:422–423.
9. For a summary of studies, see Rice, 1981:265–266.
10. Jones, 1976.
11. Engel, 1968.
12. Piaget and Inhelder, 1961.
13. Elkind, 1984:33.
14. Rice, 1981:181.
15. See, for example, Erikson, 1968.
16. Conger, 1973:379.
17. *Maclean's*, July 16, 1984.
18. Bibby, 1982.
19. Nettler, 1976:10.
20. Bibby, 1982.
21. Cited in Baughman, 1972:9.
22. Bibby, 1982.
23. "Dancing in the Dark", Bruce Springsteen, 1984.
24. See Flake-Hobson, Robinson, and Skeen, 1983:424, and Romeo, 1984:551.
25. Ushakov, 1971.
26. Cited in Flake-Hobson, Robinson, and Skeen, 1983:424.
27. Romeo, 1984.
28. See, Kagan and Squires, 1984; Halmi, Falk, and Schwartz, 1981.
29. Kagan and Squires, 1984:24.
30. Kilander, 1965:7–8.
31. Hammar, 1965.
32. Flake-Hobson, Robinson, and Skeen, 1983:425.
33. Hendry and Gullies, 1978.
34. Cited in Mauss, 1975:439.
35. Cited in Mackie, 1983b:107.
36. Associated Press release, December 5, 1984.
37. Flake-Hobson, Robinson, and Skeen, 1983:473.
38. Cited in Rice, 1981:282.
39. Bibby, 1982.
40. Lyle and Hoffman, 1972.
41. "Sad Songs Say So Much", Happenstance Limited, 1984.

42. Bibby, 1982.
43. "Metal Health", The Grand Pasha Publisher, 1983.
44. "Foolin'", Def-Lepp Music, 1983.
45. Erikson, 1968.
46. *The Globe and Mail*, October 15, 1982.
47. Solomon and Boldt, 1977:3.
48. See Rice, 1981:225–228.
49. Teicher, 1973; Solomon and Boldt, 1977:69.
50. Cited in Rice, 1981:225.
51. Teicher, 1973:133.
52. Boldt, 1982:154–155.
53. Rice, 1981:228.
54. Solomon and Boldt, 1977:82.
55. "Good Morning America", October 15, 1984.
56. Canadian Press release, October 11, 1984.

Chapter 5

1. Mitchell, 1975:113–114.
2. Elkind, 1981:87.
3. Barr, 1971:16–17.
4. Stark, 1975:240.
5. See, for example, Zelnick, Young, and Kantner, 1979; Rice, 1981:335, Herold, 1984:13–14.
6. Herold, 1984:1.
7. "Girls Just Want to Have Fun", Heroic Music, 1979.
8. "Heart and Soul", Chinnichap Publishing, Inc., 1981.
9. Herold, 1984:11.
10. MacQueen, Canadian Press release, September 14, 1984.
11. "Lick It Up", Kiss, 1983.
12. Rice, 1981:324,335.
13. Canadian Press release, May 14, 1984.
14. Canadian Press release, September 28, 1984.
15. Herold and Goodwin, 1979:245.
16. Canadian Press release, September 28, 1984.
17. Canadian Press release, November 25, 1984.
18. Leslie, 1982:380ff.
19. Cited in Leslie, 1982:384.
20. Bibby, 1982.
21. Canadian Press release, November 23, 1984.
22. *Time*, April 1984.
23. College Press Service, November 1984.
24. Canadian Press release, October 12, 1984.
25. Herold, 1984:12.

Chapter 6

1. Derived from Bibby, 1982.
2. York and Wachtel, 1982:75.
3. Flake-Hobson, Robinson, and Skeen, 1983:451.
4. Mackie, 1983a:80.
5. Flake-Hobson, Robinson, and Skeen, 1983:453.
6. Rice, 1981:283.
7. Baughman, 1972:37–38.
8. Sebald, 1968:198.

9. See, for example, Coleman, 1961.
10. Fasick, 1984:150.
11. Mackie, 1983a:76,79.
12. The Johnston Company. Synthesis of 18 Studies for Youth and Values-oriented Clients 1959–1980.
13. See, for example, Flake-Hobson, Robinson, and Skeen, 1983:450–451; Fasick, 1984.
14. Fasick, 1984:155.
15. See, for example, Conger, 1973; Cohen, 1979.
16. Rice, 1981:260.
17. Leona, 1979; cited in Flake-Hobson, Robinson, and Skeen, 1983:453.
18. Nett, 1983:290.
19. Nett, 1983:291.
20. Elkind, 1981:156.
21. Rice, 1981:41.
22. Ambert, 1980.
23. Leslie, 1982:574.
24. Nett, 1983:293.
25. Stern, Northman, and Van Slyck, 1984.
26. Rice, 1981:41.

Chapter 7

1. See Bibby and Weaver, 1985.
2. Rice, 1981:437.
3. Bibby, 1983b.
4. Bibby, 1983b.
5. Bibby, 1983b.
6. See, for example, Bibby, 1983b.
7. See Bibby, 1977.
8. Bibby, 1983b.
9. Bibby, 1984.
10. See Bibby, 1983b.
11. Berger, 1961:182.
12. See, for example, O'Doherty, 1973:86.
13. Dreyfus, 1972:71.
14. Rice, 1981:431.
15. Hauser, 1981.
16. Bibby, 1984.
17. *On Court*, interview by Pat Sinclair, August 1984:3.

Chapter 8

1. Bibby, 1983a:171.
2. Bibby, 1983a:173.
3. Bibby, 1983a:177.
4. Porter, 1977.
5. Bibby, 1979.
6. Badgley, 1984.
7. Canadian Press release, September 23, 1984.
8. Blackwell and Gessner, 1983.
9. *The Globe and Mail*, December 18, 1984.
10. *The Toronto Star*, December 2, 1984.
11. Bibby, 1979.
12. Smart, 1981.

13. Cited in Whitehead, 1984.
14. See, for example, Adrian, 1982:16; *Drug Use in America*, 1973:81.
15. Rice, 1981:142–143.
16. Canadian Press release, November 1, 1984.
17. Canadian Press release, November 1, 1984.
18. Nettler, 1976:10.
19. Fasick, 1979:123.

Chapter 9

1. Secretary of State, 1984.
2. Mackie, 1983b:114.
3. Reported in *The Lethbridge Herald*, November 21, 1984:C5.
4. Flake-Hobson, Robinson, and Skeen, 1983:455.
5. Canadian Press release, November 11, 1984.
6. Merton, 1938.
7. "Winds of Change", Lunatunes, 1982.

Chapter 10

1. Flake-Hobson, Robinson, and Skeen, 1983:44.
2. Rice, 1981:358.
3. Canadian Institute of Public Opinion, September 6, 1980.
4. Leslie, 1982:507.
5. Rice, 1981:360.
6. Cited in Rice, 1981:360.
7. Rice, 1981:373.
8. Elkind, 1981:30.
9. Ponzo, 1978. Cited in Flake-Hobson, Robinson, and Skeen, 1983:449.
10. Dreyfus, 1972:75.
11. Duvall, 1954.
12. Cited in Leslie, 1982:632.
13. Mitchell, 1975:31.
14. Elkind, 1981:71.
15. Cited in Elkind, 1981:65.
16. Cited in Robert Barr, 1971:6.
17. Clark, 1975:24.
18. Barr, 1971:7.
19. Elkind, 1981:125.
20. Elkind, 1981:124.
21. Rice, 1981:372ff; Elkind, 1981:125ff.
22. Rice, 1981:373.
23. Selected from Rice, 1981:367.
24. Boyer, 1983:44.
25. Elkind, 1984:137–138.
26. Mitchell, 1975:239.
27. Baughman, 1972:29.
28. Rice, 1981:437.
29. O'Doherty, 1973:108.
30. Elkind, 1984:215.
31. Mitchell, 1975:89.
32. Mitchell, 1975:241–246.
33. Champagne, 1984.
34. York and Wachtel, 1982.
35. Mitchell, 1975:235.
36. Elkind, 1981:199.

BIBLIOGRAPHY

ADRIAN, M.
 1982 *Statistics on Alcohol and Drug Use in Canada and Other Countries*. Toronto: Addiction Research Foundation.

AGNEW, ROBERT
 1984 "The Effect of Appearance on Personality and Behavior." *Youth and Society* 15:285–303.

AMBERT, ANNE-MARIE
 1980 *Divorce in Canada*. Toronto: Academic Press.

BADGLEY, ROBIN F., Chairman
 1984 *Sexual Offences Against Children in Canada: Summary*. Ottawa: Canadian Government Publishing Center.

BARBIERI, RICHARD E.
 1978 "A Brief History of Youth and Age." *Educational Leadership*, 35:505–508.

BARNETT, STEVE
 1984 "New Wavers Part of Conservative Rebellion." In *The Toronto Star*, February 25.

BARR, ROBERT D. (ed.)

1971 *Values and Youth*. Washington: National Council for the Social Studies.

BAUGHMAN, DALE

1972 *What Do Students Really Want?* Bloomington, Ind.: Phi Delta Kappa Educational Foundation.

BAUM, DANIEL JAY

1975 *Let Our Children Go*. Don Mills: Burns and McEachern.

BENEDICT, RUTH

1950 *Patterns of Culture*. New York: New American Library.

BERGER, PETER L.

1961 *The Noise of Solemn Assemblies*. New York: Doubleday.
1963 *Invitation to Sociology*. New York: Doubleday.

BIBBY, REGINALD W.

1977 "Religiosity in Canada: A National Survey." In Christopher Beattie and Stewart Crysdale (ed.). *Sociology Canada: Readings*. Second Edition. Toronto: Butterworth.

1979 "Consensus in Diversity: An Examination of Canadian Problem Perception." *International Journal of Comparative Sociology* 20:274–282.

1982 *Project Can80: A Second Look at Deviance, Diversity, and Devotion in Canada*. Codebook. Lethbridge: The University of Lethbridge.

1983a "The Precarious Mosaic: Divergence and Convergence in the Canadian 80s." *Social Indicators Research* 2:169–181.

1983b "Religionless Christianity: A Profile of Religion in the Canadian '80s." *Social Indicators Research* 13:1–16.

1983c "The Moral Mosaic: Sexuality in the Canadian 80s." *Social Indicators Research* 13:171–184.

1984 "Religious Encasement in Canada: An Argument for the Stability of Religion." *Social Compass*: in press.

BIBBY, REGINALD and HAROLD W. WEAVER

1985 "Cult Consumption in Canada: A Critique of Stark and Bainbridge." *Sociological Analysis*: in press.

BLACKWELL, PATRICIA L. and JOHN C. GESSNER

1983 "Fear and Trembling: An Inquiry Into Adolescent Perceptions of Living in the Nuclear Age." *Youth and Society* 15:237–255.

BLOCK, J.H., N. HAAN, and M.B. SMITH

1968 "Activism and Apathy in Contemporary Adolescents." In J.F. Adams (ed.). *Understanding Adolescence: Current Developments in Adolescent Psychology*. Boston: Allyn and Bacon. Pp. 198–231.

BOLDT, MENNO
    1982 "Normative Evaluations of Suicide and Death: A Cross-Generational Study." *Omega* 13:145–157.

BOYER, E.L.
    1983 *Highschool.* New York: Harper and Row.

BRODERICK, C.B.
    1966 "Socio-sexual Development in a Suburban Community." *The Journal of Sex Research* 2:1–24.

BROWN, FRANK B.
    1980 *The Transition of Youth to Adulthood: A Bridge Too Long.* National Commission on Youth. Boulder, Col.: Westview Press.

    1982 "Bulimia: The Latest Dieting Epidemic." *Forecast for Home Economic* 27:38.

CHAMPAGNE, ANDRÉE
    1984 *Speech by Minister of State, Youth: Throne Speech Debate, House of Commons.* Ottawa: Minister of State, Youth.

CLARK, TED
    1975 *The Oppression of Youth.* New York: Harper and Row.

COHEN, J.
    1979 "High School Subcultures and the Adult World." *Adolescence* 14:491–502.

COLEMAN, JAMES
    1961 *The Adolescent Society.* New York: Free Press.

CONGER, JOHN J
    1973 *Adolescence and Youth.* New York: Harper and Row.

COURTNEY, ALICE E. and THOMAS W. WHIPPLE
    1978 *Canadian Perspectives on Sex Stereotyping in Advertising.* Ottawa: Advisory Council on the Status of Women.

DAVIS, KINGSLEY
    1940 "The Sociology of Parent–Youth Conflict." *American Sociological Review* 20:680–684.

DREYFUS, EDWARD A.
    1972 *Youth: Search for Meaning.* Columbus: Charles Merrill.

Drug Use in America: Problem in Perspective. 1973. Second Report of the National Commission on Marihuana and Drug Abuse. Washington, D.C.: U.S. Government Printing Office.

DUVALL, EVELYN M.
    1954 *In-Laws: Pro and Con.* New York: Association Press.

ELKIND, DAVID
    1981 *The Hurried Child.* Reading, Mass.: Addison-Wesley.

    1984 *All Grown Up and No Place to Go.* Reading, Mass.: Addison-Wesley.

ELLIS, GODFREY J.
    1983 "Youth in the Electronic Environment." *Youth and Society* 15:3–12.

ENGEL, D.E.
    1968 "Education and Identity: The Functions of Questions in Religious Education." *Religious Education* 63:371–375.

ERIKSON, ERIK
    1968 *Identity and the Life Cycle.* New York: W.W. Norton.

FASICK, FRANK A.
    1979 "Acquisition of Adult Responsibilities and Rights in Adolescence." In K. Ishwaran (ed.). *Childhood and Adolescence in Canada.* Pp. 119–135.

    1984 "Parents, Peers, Youth Culture and Autonomy in Adolescence." *Adolescence* 19:143–157.

FAULKES, ZEN
    1984 "Protest Songs Stage Fighting Comeback." *The Meliorist*, University of Lethbridge, November 29:6–7.

FLAKE-HOBSON, CAROL, BRYAN E. ROBINSON, PATSY SKEEN
    1983 *Child Development and Relationships.* Reading, Mass.: Addison Wesley.

GOODMAN, PAUL
    1960 *Growing Up Absurd.* New York: Random House.

GALLUP (Canada)
    1980 CIPO Poll, September 6.

    1982 CIPO Poll, December 1.

GRABB, EDWARD G.
    1980 "Differences in Sense of Control Among French- and English-Canadian Adolescents." *Canadian Review of Sociology and Anthropology* 17:169–175.

GRINDER, ROBERT E.
    1973 *Adolescence.* New York: John Wiley.

HALMI, K.A., J.R. FALK, and E. SCHWARTZ
    1981 "Binge-Eating and Vomiting: A Survey of a College Population." *Psychological Medicine* 11:697–706.

HAMMAR, S.L.
    1965 "The Obese Adolescent." *Journal of School Health* 35:246–249.

HAUSER, JAMES
    1981 "Adolescents and Religion." *Adolescence* 16:310–320.

HAVIGHURST, ROBERT J.
    1972 *Developmental Tasks and Education.* Third Edition. New York: David McKay.

HENDRY, L.B. and P. GULLIES
   1978 "Body Type, Esteem, School, and Leisure: A Study of Overweight, Average, and Underweight Adolescents." *Journal of Youth
   and Adolescence* 7:181–195.

HEROLD, EDWARD S.
   1984 *Sexual Behaviour of Canadian Young People*. Markham:
   Fitzhenry and Whiteside.

HEROLD, EDWARD S. and MARILYN R. GOODWIN
   1979 "The Adoption of Oral Contraceptives Among Adolescent
   Females: Reference Group Influence." In K. Ishwaran (ed.). *Childhood and Adolescence in Canada*. Pp. 232–248.

HOBART, CHARLES W.
   1981 "Sources of Egalitarianism in Young Unmarried Canadians."
   Canadian Journal of Sociology 6:261–282.

ISHWARAN, K. and KWOK CHAN
   1979 "The Socialization of Rural Adolescents." In K. Ishwaran
   (ed.). *Childhood and Adolescence in Canada*. Pp. 97–118.

KAGAN, DONA M. and ROSE L. SQUIRES
   1984 "Eating Disorders Among Adolescents: Patterns and Preva-
   lence." *Adolescence* 19:15–29.

JONES, S.S.
   1976 "High School Social Status as a Historical Process." *Adolescence*
   11:327–333.

KERR, ANTHONY
   1964 *Youth of Europe*. Chester Springs, Pa.: Dufour Editions.

KILANDER, H. FREDERICK
   1965 "Adolescents Fail on Food Facts." *PTA Magazine* 59:7–8.

LAMBERT, W.E., A. YACKLEY, and R.N. HEIN
   1971 "Child Training Values of English-Canadian and French-
   Canadian Parents." *Canadian Journal of Behavioural Science* 3:
   217–236.

LARSON, REED and ROBERT KUBEY
   1983 "Television and Music: Contrasting Media in Adolescent
   Life." *Youth and Society* 15:13–31.

LEVINE, HAROLD G. and STEVEN H. STUMPF
   1983 "Statements of Fear Through Cultural Symbols." *Youth and
   Society* 14:417–435.

LESLIE, GERALD R.
   1982 *The Family in Social Context*. Fifth Edition. New York: Oxford
   University Press.

LYLE, J. and H. HOFFMAN

1972 "Children's Use of Television and Other Media." In E. Rubenstein et al. (eds.). *Television and Social Behaviour, Volume 4.* Washington, D.C.: Government Printing Office.

MACKIE, MARLENE

1983a "Socialization." Chapter 3 in Robert Hagedorn (ed.). *Sociology.* Toronto: Holt, Rinehart, and Winston.

1983b "Gender Relations." Chapter 4 in Robert Hagedorn (ed.). *Sociology.* Toronto: Holt, Rinehart, and Winston.

MAUSS, ARMAND L.

1975 *Social Problems as Social Movements.* Philadelphia: Lippincott.

McCORMACK, THELMA

1979 "Television and the Changing Cultures of Childhood." In K. Ishwaran (ed.). *Childhood and Adolescence in Canada.* Pp. 302–321.

McLUHAN, MARSHALL

1964 *Understanding Media.* New York: Mentor.

MEAD, MARGARET

1950 *Coming of Age in Samoa.* New York: New American Library.

MERTON, ROBERT

1938 "Social Structure and Anomie." *American Sociological Review* 3:672–682.

MILLER, DEREK

1969 *The Age Between: Adolescents in a Disturbed Society.* Cornmarket: Hutchinson.

MITCHELL, JOHN J.

1975 *The Adolescent Predicament.* Toronto: Holt, Rinehart, and Winston.

NETT, EMILY M.

1983 "The Family." Chapter 9 in Robert Hagedorn (ed.). *Sociology.* Toronto: Holt, Rinehart, and Winston.

NETTLER, GWYNN

1976 *Social Concerns.* Toronto: McGraw-Hill.

O'DOHERTY, EAMONN F.

1973 *The Religious Formation of the Adolescent.* New York: Alba House.

PIAGET, JEAN and B. INHELDER

1961 *The Growth of Logical Thinking From Childhood to Adolescence.* New York: Basic Books.

POMEROY, WARDELL B.

1968 *Boys and Sex.* New York: Delacorte Press.

POOLE, MILLICENT E.
    1984 "The Schools Adolescents Would Like." *Adolescence* 19:447–458.

PORTER, JOHN
    1977 "Ethnic Pluralism in Canadian Perspective." In Christopher Beattie and Stewart Crysdale (eds.). *Sociology Canada: Readings.* Toronto: Butterworth.

RAMSEY, CHARLES E.
    1967 *Problems of Youth.* Belmont, Calif.: Wadsworth.

ROKEACH, MILTON
    1973 *The Nature of Human Values.* New York: Free Press.

ROMEO, FELICIA R.
    1984 "Adolescence, Sexual Conflict, and Anorexia Nervosa." *Adolescence* 19:551–555.

RICE, F. PHILIP
    1981 *The Adolescent: Development, Relationships, and Culture.* Third Edition. Boston: Allyn and Bacon.

SEBALD, HANS
    1968 *Adolescence: A Sociological Analysis.* New York: Appleton-Century-Crofts.
    1981 "Adolescents' Concept of Popularity and Unpopularity, Comparing 1960 with 1976." *Adolescence* 16:187–193.

SHAINESS, N.A.
    1961 "A Re-evaluation of Some Aspects of Femininity Through a Study of Menstruation: A Preliminary Report." *Comprehensive Psychiatry* 2:20–26.

SMART, REGINALD
    1981 *Preliminary Report of Alcohol and Other Drug Use Among Ontario Students in 1981, and Changes Since 1977 and 1979.* Toronto: Addiction Research Foundation.

SOLOMON, MARK and MENNO BOLDT
    1977 *Report on Suicide. Phase One: Youth Suicide.* Edmonton: Department of Social Services and Community Health, Province of Alberta.

SONTAG, SUSAN
    1972 "The Double Standard of Aging." *Saturday Review*, September 23.

STARK, RODNEY
    1975 *Social Problems.* Del Mar, Calif.: CRM Books.

STERN, MARILYN, JOHN NORTHMAN, and MICHAEL R. VAN SLYNCK
    1984 "Father Absence and Adolescent 'Problem Behaviors': Alcohol Consumption, Drug Use and Sexual Activity." *Adolescence* 74:301–312.

TEICHER, JOSEPH D.
    1973 "A Solution to the Chronic Problem of Living: Adolescent Attempted Suicide." In J.C. Schoolar (ed.). *Current Issues in Adolescent Psychiatry*. New York: Brunner-Mazel. Pp. 129–147.

TOMAN, WALTER
    1961 *Family Constellation*. New York: Springer.

USHAKOV, G.K.
    1971 "Anorexia Nervosa." In J.G. Howells (ed.). *Modern Perspectives in Adolescent Psychiatry*. New York: Brunner-Mazel. Pp. 274–289.

WESTHUES, KENNETH
    1975 "Intergenerational Conflict in the Sixties." In Samuel Clark, Paul Grayson, and Linda Grayson. *Prophecy and Protest: Social Movements in Twentieth Century Canada*. Toronto: Gage. Pp. 387–408.

WHITEHEAD, PAUL C.
    1984 *Young Drinkers: A Review of Recent Canadian Studies*. Ottawa: Health Promotion Directorate, Health and Welfare.

YACOUBIAN, J.H. and R.S. LOURIE
    1973 "Suicide and Attempted Suicide in Children and Adolescents." In S.L. Copel (ed.). *Pathology of Childhood and Adolescence*. New York: Basic Books. Pp. 149–165.

YORK, PHYLLIS and DAVID, and TED WACHTEL
    1982 *Toughlove*. New York: Doubleday.

ZELNIK, M., K. YOUNG, and J.F. KANTNER
    1979 "Probabilities of Intercourse and Conception Among U.S. Teenage Women." *Family Planning Perspectives* 11:177–183.